RECOLLECTIONS
and
RECONSIDERATIONS

RECOLLECTIONS
and
RECONSIDERATIONS

Margaret R. Miles

CASCADE *Books* • Eugene, Oregon

RECOLLECTIONS AND RECONSIDERATIONS

Copyright © 2018 Margaret R. Miles. All rights reserved. Except for brief quotations in critical publications or reviews, no part of this book may be reproduced in any manner without prior written permission from the publisher. Write: Permissions, Wipf and Stock Publishers, 199 W. 8th Ave., Suite 3, Eugene, OR 97401.

Cascade Books
An Imprint of Wipf and Stock Publishers
199 W. 8th Ave., Suite 3
Eugene, OR 97401

www.wipfandstock.com

PAPERBACK ISBN: 978-1-5326-4057-5
HARDCOVER ISBN: 978-1-5326-4058-2
EBOOK ISBN: 978-1-5326-4059-9

Cataloguing-in-Publication data:

Names: Miles, Margaret R.—(Margaret Ruth),—1937–, author.

Title: Recollections and reconsiderations / Margaret R. Miles.

Description: Eugene, OR : Cascade Books, 2018 | Includes bibliographical references and index.

Identifiers: ISBN 978-1-5326-4057-5 (paperback) | ISBN 978-1-5326-4058-2 (hardcover) | ISBN 978-1-5326-4059-9 (ebook)

Subjects: LCSH: Miles, Margaret R.—(Margaret Ruth),—1937–.

Classification: BX4827.M55 A3 2018 (paperback) | BX4827.M55 A3 (ebook)

Manufactured in the U.S.A.   12/14/18

For my dear longtime friends, Drs. William and Sally Rankin, "doers of the word and not hearers only" (James 1:22)

Thou shalt remember all the way by which the Lord thy God has led thee through this wildness.

—Deuteronomy 8.2

Contents

Acknowledgments | ix
Preface | xi

Part I
Chapter 1: Introduction | 3
Chapter 2: First Publications, 1979 to 1981 | 11
Chapter 3: Tenure, 1982 to 1985 | 25

Part II
Chapter 4: Teaching and Writing, 1986 to 1996 | 41
Chapter 5: Administration, 1996 to 2002 | 74

Part III
Chapter 6: Retirement Part I, 2002 to 2011 | 91
Chapter 7: Retirement Part II, 2011 to 2017 | 106

Part IV
Chapter 8: Reading Augustine Reading Augustine | 125
Chapter 9: Recollections and Reconsiderations | 131
Chapter 10: "My Weight is My Love" | 143

Bibliography | 149
Index | 157

Acknowledgments

A SCHOLAR IS UTTERLY dependent on the quality of the conversations in which she participates. Critical friends question, make suggestions, even recall obvious connections that I easily forget when working alone at my desk. I am grateful for the myriad conversations—with students, colleagues and friends—I have been privileged to enjoy across many years. Our inherited image of the scholar, alone at his desk, (now) hunched over a hot computer, his ideas funneled into his brain from rich intellectual ether, is not consonant with my experience. This manuscript owes its existence to thoughtful conversations with Judith Berling, Frank Burch Brown, Leslie Ewing, China Galland and Corey Fischer, Steve Hitchcock, Martin Laird, Corrie Lassen, and Bill and Sally Rankin.

I am very grateful for my editor, Charlie Collier, who has generously welcomed my writings for many years. I am also indebted to the skillful people at Wipf and Stock who manage the intricate details that make for a well-presented book.

Preface

LECTURING ON THE HEBREW prophet Jonah, Martin Luther—a good story teller—describes Jonah's experience in vivid detail. He wants his hearers to *personalize* Jonah's experience, to live every minute, every second, with breathless attentiveness, to *experience* Jonah's anxiety. Luther comments:

> Because we are only spectators of tragedies of this sort, they do not appear to us so great and so terrible as they really are. But if we were experiencing them ourselves in our consciousness, we would understand what it is to feel God's wrath against oneself and what that faith is which even in the middle of wrath holds on to God as merciful and kind.[1]

Luther takes his time narrating the back story that led to Jonah being thrown into the sea from the storm-tossed ship. As the "whale" approaches, he again reminds his hearers not to "think of the later Jonah when he is delivered." Rather, he instructs them to relive the moment when "the poor, lost, and dying Jonah [saw] the whale open its mouth wide and he beheld sharp teeth that stood upright all around like pointed pillars or beams and he peered down the wide cellar entrance to the belly."

Luther had a reason for dwelling at length and in detail on the "otherwise insignificant story" of Jonah.[2] His dramatic story made a theological point: Jonah's mortal terror is *the* condition, he says—the only condition—in which God hears and responds to sinners' cries for mercy.[3] Moreover, Jonah's story reiterates Luther's own autobiography. Characterizing his "wildly aroused and disturbed conscience" as a young monk, Luther says

---

1. Luther, *Lectures on Jonah*, 4.
2. Luther, *Lectures on Jonah*, 4.
3. "He is a God who looks into the depths and helps *only* the poor, despised, afflicted, miserable, forsaken, and those who are nothing," Luther, *Magnificat*, 300.

that if he had continued in the harsh ascetic practices with which he attempted to attract God's mercy, he would have killed himself. He recalls his own utterly despairing cry to God with a metaphor: "The rope breaks where it is tightest."[4]

Luther describes the perspective necessary for hearing the story of Jonah and other Hebrew Bible stories *in the life*. The protagonists, he said, *did not know*—as do readers—the outcome of the story. Jonah in the belly of the great fish, imagining its stomach acids beginning to eat his skin, did not know that he would be rescued. Just so, we live the events of our lives *not knowing* the outcome. I did not *know* the positive tenure decision; I did *not know* that I would be able to publish the next article or book; I did *not know* that a dear grandchild would have a doctorate and teach at a university; I did *not know* that a beloved son would stop drinking.[5] At age eighty I know the "end" of my story, so I am tempted to forget the emotions—from gut-wrenching anxiety to vivid delight—that accompanied its process. Not the least benefit of reviewing my publications while *knowing* outcomes is that the exercise produces a sense of profound gratitude for the richness of the mixture, for all of it—the indefatigable work, the anxiety, and the joy.

I have been amazed to observe on several academic occasions that most scholars' autobiographies focus on the influence of several teachers and a few books. Nothing is said about the people and events, the joys, losses, and disappointments that informed and directed the scholar's attention, energy, and heated interests. The wives, children, and friends who nourished and encouraged a scholar are apparently not considered an important aspect of his life and work; neither emotions nor "fellow pilgrims" are part of the story academics tell ourselves about our lives. However if, as Plotinus taught, "life and thought are one," then the omission of *life* in a scholar's autobiography must offer a distorted picture of *thought*.[6] The *life*

---

4. Luther, *Lectures on Jonah*, 79. At the terminus of mental and physical exhaustion, Luther understood God's justice, a concept that had previously enraged him: "The just shall live *by faith*."

5. My son's alcoholism has been a leitmotiv of my semi-autobiographical publications. After he had been homeless for almost two years, in 2016 he agreed to enter a three-month detox and rehab program. Presently, mid-2017, he has not had a drink in well over a year. He is damaged in mind and body by forty years of alcoholism, but I am cautiously hopeful that, at fifty-eight years old, he can still enjoy some good years.

6. I puzzled at length over a more accurate expression of this "oneness," as did Plotinus, who complained frequently in the *Enneads* of the inadequacy of language to describe what is real. See my *Plotinus on Body and Beauty*, 27–28, for a discussion of Plotinus's complaint.

Preface

of the "life story" is missing. I am not as talented a story teller as Luther, but I hope nevertheless that my reflections will prompt readers generously to imagine the *life* of my story.

Today, 18 May 2016 is my seventy-ninth birthday and the beginning of my eightieth year—today I begin this reflective retrospective.[7]

---

7. I do not comment on some articles that became preambles to a book.

PART I

Chapter 1

Introduction

Whoever reads my books in the order in which they were written will likely find out how much progress I have made with my writing.[1]

For me, Lord, certainly this is hard labor, hard labor inside myself, and I have become to myself a piece of difficult ground, not to be worked over without much sweat.[2]

I confess, then, that I attempt to be one of those who write because they have made some progress, and who, by means of writing, make further progress.[3]

1

SEVERAL YEARS BEFORE HIS death in 430 CE, Augustine undertook to review his published works, "commenting briefly on their purpose, contents, and mistakes."[4] He did so, he wrote in a letter to a fellow bishop, because "anything that offends me might offend others."[5] However, he was distracted from rereading his writings by a heated correspondence with Julian

---

1. Quotations not footnoted are from the publication discussed. Augustine, *Retractationes*, prol., 3.
2. Augustine, *Confessions*, 10.16.
3. Augustine, *Epistula*, 143.2.
4. Brown, *Augustine*, 442.
5. Augustine, *Epistula*, 224.2.

of Eclanum over the operation of God's grace in the life of a Christian.[6] He did not return to reviewing his many treatises, letters, and sermons as he intended. He finished his critical review in 427 CE, having reviewed ninety-three of his publications.

James O'Donnell has proposed that Augustine's *Retractationes*, written thirty years after his *Confessions*,[7] should be thought of as volume two of his autobiography. In *Confessions*, Augustine vividly narrates his intense struggle to understand and accept catholic Christianity. His narrative concludes at age thirty-three; the following decades of his strenuous activity as a bishop, author, and pastor are not discussed in detail.[8] Read as Augustine's autobiography, volume 2, *Retractationes* describes the extraordinary life and thinking of an authoritative fifth-century North African bishop.

Augustine had several agenda in writing autobiographically. Perhaps the most intimate of these agenda was detecting and describing *to himself* the story of his own life. The story that emerged was that he was "at all times on fire to meditate on the law of his god [sic], day and night."[9] Yet Augustine's readers notice different agenda. James O'Donnell notices the "self-indulgence" and "self-absorption" of the *Confessions*,[10] its "self-revelation mixed with self-concealment."[11] In volume 2 of his autobiography, the same reviewer writes, "Augustine invents the story of Augustine the bishop... [effectively] "replacing the living, breathing, quarreling cleric with Augustine the author."[12]

2

Like Augustine's *Confessions*, *Augustine and the Fundamentalist's Daughter*, volume one of my autobiography, describes the struggles of my youth, only briefly mentioning my teaching and writing career after 1978. *Recollections and Reconsiderations*, volume 2, considers my publications as they reveal

---

6. Julian believed that every person is given at birth enough grace to sustain her through life; Augustine insisted that a person is dependent at each moment of life for renewed grace.
7. O'Donnell, *Augustine, Sinner and Saint*, 315.
8. O'Donnell, *Augustine, Sinner and Saint*, 317.
9. O'Donnell, *Augustine, Sinner and Saint*, 319.
10. O'Donnell, *Augustine, Sinner and Saint*, 141.
11. O'Donnell, *Augustine, Sinner and Saint*, 318.
12. O'Donnell, *Augustine, Sinner and Saint*, 319.

Introduction

and mirror my life from 1978 to 2017, beginning with the publication of my doctoral dissertation in 1979.

These reflections might be considered the story of the life of my mind, except that I do not accept a model of human being in which the activities of "something called body" and "something called soul or mind" can be clearly distinguished.[13] One of the greatest gifts of my life was the discovery of an alternative to the classical model of "person" in which components of unequal value are stacked hierarchically. I refer to Maxine Sheets-Johnstone's understanding of person as an "intelligent body," *one entity*, not analyzable into components. Of which, more later.

The examination of one's own writings is not an easy venture: Augustine was "loath to admit that he was ever distinctly *wrong* on a point of substance."[14] I, however, notice multiple points at which I lacked important concepts that I understood only much later. For example, throughout my doctoral dissertation, *Augustine on the Body*, and for at least a decade following, I referred to "the body." I have come to understand that there is no such entity. No one ever saw or touched "the body," a genderless, sexless, entity, unmarked by skin color, social location, health, age, nourishment, and a number of other variables. From approximately 1990 forward my preferred usage is to delete the article, thereby, I hope, deleting the suggestion that body is—or ever can be while the person is alive—a stand-alone entity. Intelligent bodies, beautiful and interesting in their ideas, their particularity, singularity, and plethora of experiences, are what we see and touch.

Rereading my early publications reveals some continuities and some changes in my *habits of thinking*. Habits of thinking are more resistant to change than are ideas. Virtually inaccessible to consciousness, they are preferences for certain *kinds* of explanation.[15] Habits of thought are deeply embedded in the language we use. Notice, for example, how very difficult it is to think of, or refer to, oneness without imaging a union of two or more entities.[16]

---

13. Sheets-Johnstone, *Corporeal Turn*, 20.

14. O'Donnell, *Augustine, Sinner and Saint*, 318.

15. Many twenty-first-century scholars have a committed predilection for *political or social/cultural* explanations; they tend to doubt the validity of *religious* motivations, even when the subjects of their study explicitly acknowledge religious motivation.

16. Sheets-Johnstone, referring to body and mind, insists "there is no 'they.'" *Corporeal Turn*, 20.

Recollections and Reconsiderations

Hannah Arendt suggested that the only requirement of Socratic thinking is *self-consistency*.[17] But is it possible to eliminate self-contradiction? How often do one's sincerest intentions and efforts produce the aimed-for *effects*?[18] The goal of self-consistency must assume that the "true self" is a single entity that can be discovered and adhered to. It ignores counter-evidence of the existence of multiple selves constituted by different loyalties and values. If we assume the "multiple selves" hypothesis, *can* an author, even with the best intentions, review her/his life honestly without mixed feelings and judgments? I have not been able to.

Jean Jacques Rousseau said that he endeavored to write about himself "without ostentation and without weakness."[19] I am not persuaded that he succeeded in this goal, but I am advised by his effort. The problems endemic to such a project appear immediately. To suggest only a few: memory cannot be trusted;[20] only one perspective is represented in descriptions of circumstances involving several or many perspectives; external events can be recalled easily, but to retrieve and relive the attendant *emotions* is more difficult and occasionally painful.

A "critical" examination is approximately the opposite of a "judgmental" reconstruction. A critical approach seeks to reveal *why* I had an inadequate grasp of a complex idea. It must include the circumstances that both enabled *and* limited my understanding, as well as the resources I had *at the time*. I try to avoid one trick often found in autobiographies, namely, contrasting my present sagaciousness with my earlier foolishness. I may marvel, *marvel,* on occasion at how stupid and wrong I was, but as preamble to exploring why I thought or acted as I did. If I thought stupidly and acted wrongly, I seek to understand why. Augustine is not my model for this kindness to my young self; he was judgmental of his youthful self.

This generosity attempts to compensate for the harshly judgmental view of myself and others with which I grew up. Many hours of education

---

17. Arendt, *Thinking*, 186.

18. "I've always thought of wholeness and integration as necessary myths. We're fragmented beings who cement ourselves together, but there are always cracks. Living with the cracks is part of being, well, healthy." Hustvedt, *Sorrows*, 139.

19. Rousseau, *Confessions*.

20. "Memory. . . is not a storehouse of fixed imaged and words, but a dynamic association network in the brain that is never quiet and is subject to revision each time we retrieve an old picture or old words." Husvedt, *Sorrows*, 80. Also "The falsification of memory—the adjustment, abbreviation, invention, and omission of experience –is common to us all, it is the business of psychic life." McGrath, *Trauma*, 46.

Introduction

and psychotherapy over a period of many years, and many alternative models—found in books and in observation of others—were needed to overcome my self-judgments. I came to understand that the scriptural injunction, "love your neighbor as yourself," can be read as a simple declarative sentence: "You [do] love the neighbor as yourself." I learned that if I am harsh with myself, I will inevitably be harsh with others. My mantra has evolved to: "I did the best I could—and it wasn't enough," thus forgiving myself while nevertheless acknowledging that I was not lazy or neglectful; I did my best, but sadly, my best was not—*could not have been*—"enough" in the situation.

Difficult and sometimes painful as it is, I highly recommend to scholars in retirement the exercise of reviewing one's own publications. There are substantial benefits; for example, one is occasionally surprised and pleased by one's perspicacity. Alternatively, one is humbled by its lack. Although humility may not immediately appear to be a great benefit, Augustine valued humility very highly, going so far as to say, "The way is firstly humility, secondly humility, and thirdly humility."[21] But the greatest benefit is that a review of one's life's work *quilts* that work into a body, a *corpus*—not simply one thing after another. The stresses of an academic life of publication and teaching—such as standing before a roomful of intelligent students, trying to sound knowledgeable for fifty minutes at a time—require that, having completed one project, one must quickly begin the next. There is no time to reflect on an earlier project. Only when viewed consecutively and thoughtfully do one's writings form a whole, one article or book building on, or correcting, another. The integrity of the *corpus*, characterized by consistent values and loyalties, reveals what one *stood for* as a scholar.[22] Contemplation and life can be recognized as one.

> *If, then, the truest life is life by thought, and is the same as the truest*
> *thought, then the truest thought lives,*
> *and contemplation, and the object of contemplation*
> *at this level, is living and life, and the two together are one.*
>   Plotinus, *Enneads*, 3.8.3

---

21. Augustine, *Epistula*, 118; he described humility as the emotional posture in which learning can occur.

22. At the age of 100, the African-American scholar and activist Anna Julia Cooper said, "It doesn't matter so much what you said, or even what you did. It matters what you stood for."

Recollections and Reconsiderations

The above quotation comes from a third-century Platonic philosopher, Plotinus. Plotinus insists that life and thought are one; notice, however, that he must begin with the assumption that life and thought are distinguishable entities. Language does not help. He must use many words to assert that "the two together are one." He cannot simply say that life/thought is *consanguineous*. Even the words by which we seek to overcome the separation of life and thought, words like "unity" and "relationship," begin by positing two separate entities connected by a bridge.[23] The language of description is not the language of reality; description must *analyze the parts* of an entity; the whole cannot be described, but must simply be *invoked*.

The inability of language to *say what one means* is the first problem of the historian. Plotinus, speaking of his most important topics, "the Good" and "matter," complains that words do not accurately represent his meaning; one must understand "as if" (*hoion*) when he speaks, he says, "for one is unable to speak of them as one should."[24] Other problems also appear, whether one attempts to describe one's own life or the history of nations and generations. In what follows I consider several of the most prominent difficulties.

Despite our best efforts accurately to represent the past, all accounts of history, including descriptions of the present, contain inevitable elements of fiction. There are several reasons why this is so.

1) We do not have access to everything we need to know to create an accurate picture. We have only the records and documents that people of the past chose to preserve.

2) Therefore, the evidence we have is both partial and biased; for example, evidence is preserved almost entirely by literate (educated, privileged) men.

3) Our own prejudices, biases, and assumptions direct what we see when we examine evidence. We organize stories of the past according to "what we have learned how to see."[25] The more integrated, cohesive,

---

23. Augustine was constrained to use the language of body and soul he inherited. In his treatise *De trinitate* he found it impossible to explain the Christian belief in "one God in three persons" until he lit on an anthropological model—one person with three *activities*, memory, understanding, and will.

24. Plotinus, *Ennead*, 6.8.13; 6.8.18.

25. Donna Haraway's phrase; her point is that "we are responsible for what we have learned how to see." *Writing on the Body*, 283.

and persuasive the story we tell, the more the complexity of the past—the past, "boiling with life," as Plotinus put it—has been winnowed out.

4) Despite the scarcity of historical evidence, there is usually still too much evidence to form a coherent story. Historians (and autobiographers) must be skilled in "data reduction," that is, in ignoring evidence that does not support—or actively conflicts with—the story s/he seeks to tell. A best-selling historical book is popular because of the historian's data-reduction skills; by careful selection she builds a story that makes past events and people accessible, recognizable, and understandable *according to present perspectives*.[26] In addition,

5) Historians' values influence their work For example, I think that a religious life should challenge and offer *alternatives* to gender socialization rather than reinforcing secular expectations. Yet devotional manuals address and correct male socialization to aggressive action, but leave intact—or vigorously support—female socialization. They repeatedly remind their readers (without gender distinction) to feel concern for others' needs. But many or most women are socialized to attend constantly and exclusively to "the needs of *others*," ignoring their own needs. The blessing of a meal—"keep us mindful of the needs of others"—is misdirected to full-time caregivers who may need to *forget* the needs of others for a short time while they eat! In short, the common assumptions of Christian devotional literature that "one size fits all" is inaccurate and potentially damaging. Indeed, a word, a symbol, a practice, or an image that attracts a particular individual or society, may be confining, even dangerous, for another individual, another society, or another time or place.

Responsible history demonstrates simultaneously the resources *and* the problems noticed by the historian. *Both* should be brought to readers' attention. Often the beauty and the problems are difficult to unravel. Ardent lovers of Christianity (among whom I count myself) should also be its critics.

---

26. Because of the secularity of American society, historians often ignore historical peoples' religious motivation, even when sources explicitly claim it.

Recollections and Reconsiderations

4

During my career as an historical theologian, I dreamed of designing a doctoral program in which students would be trained *both* as historians and as theologians. The tools and skills of each differ, but both are necessary to recover a *more* accurate understanding of historical authors and circumstances. Historians need training in the use of archives; theologians must be able to comprehend ideas in all their subtlety, nuance, and (strong) power. Unfortunately, this kind of expertise would require *either* two doctorates, one in social and intellectual history, and one in philosophical theology, *or* the close cooperation of two departments unaccustomed to working together. Both departments would be likely to consider the student's training lacking in the full rigor of their own methods and skills.

I have several agenda in *Recollections and Reconsiderations*: chapters 2–7 reflect on my publications chronologically. Chapter 8 offers a critical review of Augustine's *Retractationes*. In chapter 9, informed by more than half a century of reading, thinking, writing about, and teaching the history of Christianity, I comment on some perennial problems I notice in the history of Christianity. Chapter 10 concludes by acknowledging the story I tell myself about my life.

Chapter 2

First Publications, 1979 to 1981

The various productions of an author date from various moments, and cannot be strictly considered to have the same origin, the same author.[1]

1

I WAS A STUDENT at San Francisco State University during the Fall 1966 semester while SFSU was lively with student demonstrations against President S. I. Hiakawa's policies. Professor Matthew Evans advised me to stay out of the fray, to continue my education with reading courses rather than classes. My interest in Augustine began in a reading course with Professor Evans.

I was immediately attracted by Augustine's passion and the power and beauty of his language—even in translation—in his *Confessions*.[2] But in reading around, I noticed that many twentieth-century authors blamed Augustine as the source of Western "dualism" and hatred of body and sex. I was puzzled that an author considered esteemed and authoritative by centuries of Christians could be presently cast as a villain. Then I read Peter Brown's magisterial *Augustine of Hippo* and was intrigued by

---

1. Gallop, *Daughter's Seduction*, 105.
2. I continued to prefer Rex Warner's English translation for Mentor-Omega Books throughout my teaching career. Language—words—can be translated along a continuum from pallid to vivid, and Warner consistently translated Augustine's colorful language toward the strong end of the continuum. In my judgment his translations most accurately preserved Augustine's vivid—even, sometimes, violent—Latin.

the complexity of Brown's blending of Augustine's social, institutional, and political history, Scripture, classical influences, and personal experience. Together, Brown's *Augustine* and Augustine's *Confessions* convinced me that I needed to learn more in order to begin to approach an adequate understanding of Augustine. I decided to study Augustine at the Graduate Theological Union, Berkeley.

By the time I applied and was accepted at GTU, my husband and I had moved to a small California gold-rush town in the Sierra foothills where we taught at Columbia Community College. With an MA in Humanities, the college administration apparently thought I should be able to teach anything from Semantics to World Religions. I scrambled to keep one step ahead of the students. Moreover, after studying all summer for a course I was scheduled to teach in the Fall, courses often changed at the last moment, based on registration. In my classrooms were young students whose parents supported them as long as they were in school, and older firemen, nurses, and others who received pay raises for continuing education. Students often seemed to dare me to interest them in the subject of the class.

I taught in Columbia three days a week, and commuted to Berkeley for seminars and libraries twice a week—140 miles each way. While I drove, I memorized vocabulary in the languages I needed in order to qualify at "marked proficiency"—Latin, Greek, and German; I had already tested successfully in French after refurbishing my high-school French. Sometimes I wonder how I managed such a schedule. Then I remember: I was young, and I was very excited about what I was learning. As Augustine put it: *Inardescimus et imus* ("We are inflamed and we go").[3] Yes!

I completed course requirements and began to write my dissertation within three years. I did not get a teaching position in 1977, the year I received my doctorate, but the Church Divinity School of the Pacific, the Episcopal school with which I was affiliated, generously allowed me—against the rules—to continue as a Teaching Assistant during the following year. CDSP also gave me a parking space, for which I was profoundly grateful; the difficulty of parking on streets around the University of California might well have put me over the top in terms of difficulty.

---

3. Augustine, *Confessions*, 13.9.

First Publications, 1979 to 1981

2

> We must bend easily lest we break.[4]

One day I noticed a letter posted on a bulletin board advertising an entrance-level position at the Harvard University Divinity School. Admonishing myself that I had nothing to lose, I responded. To shorten a long story, I was hired and arrived in Cambridge, Massachusetts, to begin my teaching duties in Fall 1978.

Professor George Hunston Williams had retired, and I was hired primarily to teach History of Christian Thought, a course that should be—and had been—taught by the most experienced and knowledgeable professor on the faculty. The course was daunting, but it was also a great gift to me; each time I taught it I dug deeper into the authors and circumstances of the Christian movement. Teachers' best-kept secret is that teaching not only requires but also facilitates learning—the teacher's learning, that is. To paraphrase Samuel Johnson, nothing concentrates the mind as effectively as knowing that you must shortly stand up in front of a large number of intelligent students, hoping not to sound stupid or ill-prepared. "History of Christian Thought" came to be my most gratifying course, largely because of its huge potential for (my) learning.[5]

Suddenly I was not a graduate assistant lecturing once during the semester and preparing the whole semester for this lecture. Now I had a lecture or seminar every day of the week. Moreover, from focusing intensively on one historical situation—late Roman antiquity—and one author—Augustine of Hippo—I was scrolling rapidly through the history of Christianity from about 100 CE (New Testament scholars had the earlier time covered), to the death of Rousseau (where others picked up with Kant and took over modern European philosophy and theology). As each lecture approached I prepared frantically, and for about a month I vomited before each lecture. I reported this to my doctor, who told me that sports players who suffer from pre-game anxiety do this regularly. "It's a non-harmful way to relieve tension," she said.

Two decades earlier, when I was twenty-two, I had suffered from an ulcer that threatened to perforate. When I returned to college at the age of

---

4. Augustine, *Epistula*, 104.3.11.

5. Most academics enter the teaching profession because we love to learn. But we often park ourselves in a narrow specialization in which, at best, we fine tune our knowledge; we no longer expose ourselves to fundamentally new knowledge.

twenty-six, the ulcer had vanished and never recurred. My early teaching experience—pressure frequently escalating to panic—might have prompted a recurrence of the ulcer, but it didn't. Its root cause was boredom, I think, a condition that, in my case, was cured by intellectual excitement. Abraham Maslow said, "A capacity is a need." My mind, unused, became a need not met. No matter how strenuous my circumstances, using my mind kept the ulcer at bay.

Two senior colleagues came to greet me the evening I arrived In Cambridge, Massachusetts. Pretending to joke, one of them remarked, "You won't be here long if you don't publish!" I had not published a word and this "welcome" frightened me, but it also got my attention and (much later) I came to appreciate it. Lacking this realistic warning, teaching, with all its insistent immediacy, would almost certainly have absorbed all my attention and energy, leaving none for publishing.

During my second week of teaching a student told me that several women had dropped my course. Why? I asked. The student replied that they (rightly) perceived that I was not a feminist. This was apparent to them because I did not dress in the mandatory uniform of late-1970s East Coast feminists—jeans and hiking boots. I was devastated, but I did not dress differently. Instead I began to read, endeavoring to understand current feminist conversation.

I was anxious most of the time during my first several years of teaching at Harvard Divinity School. But I was also excited. I was keenly aware of being under scrutiny (familiar from childhood), both from students and colleagues. And I *knew* that I was not "good enough," smart enough, knowledgeable enough, to be lecturing across the history of Christianity. Also, a California resident for my adult life until then, I was unaccustomed to the Boston cold; keeping warm seemed to require a good deal of physical energy. My landlord controlled the heat in my apartment; it was never enough. On many winter mornings, I dressed, then put my bathrobe on over my clothes, exchanging my down bathrobe for my down coat at the door as I departed. On one of these mornings I took off my bathrobe and put on my coat forgetting that I had not put on a skirt. Halfway to my office, thinking about the lecture I would give in a short while, I began to feel an unfamiliar coolness about my legs. No skirt, only tights! I turned around and went home to finish dressing, grateful that I had noticed the omission before I took off my coat in my classroom. Another morning, preoccupied, I almost stepped off a curb as a large truck speeded by.

I fell in love. My love, whom I married three years later, was a recently divorced tenured professor at another school. He knew my colleagues and was intimately familiar with the rigors of academic life. He considered students and colleagues alike as interesting, not intimidating, "folks," an attitude I attempted to appropriate. It took awhile. Gradually I learned to remind myself that *if* I knew the stories of the people whose faces I saw in my classroom, I would understand that each of them had struggles, insecurities, and fears as well as intelligence. As students told me their stories, I learned the truth of that assumption and was helped to see their faces no longer as disapproving or judgmental.

3

Augustine on the Body (1979)

I began to look for something I might be able to publish. The only possibility was my dissertation, which sought to demonstrate that Augustine's understanding of the meaning and value of "the body" challenged the classical model in which body's primary philosophical function was to exhibit, by contrast, the greater beauty and worth of the soul. I argued that as Augustine's thought matured, his esteem for body changed. From agreeing with Plotinus that "the soul is the person,"[6] he came to say, "I want to be healed wholly because I am the whole."[7]

Augustine recognized that the classical model of person was not adequate for the religion of the Incarnation, the "word made flesh." The model he inherited featured unequal entities, hierarchically arranged according to value. Body was understood to be on the lowest level; rational soul topped and dominated the components. Woven through Augustine's letters, sermons, and treatises are quiet revisions of body's value that I eagerly gathered in my attempt to "prove" his focused interest in revising the classical model. I was onto something, but my understanding was partial.

The influence of Augustine's intellectual and cultural surroundings was strong, almost irresistible, as it is for anyone. The excitement of his intellectual culture, articulated by Plato and still prominent in the popular Platonism of Augustine's time, lay in *distinguishing* body and soul/mind, in rescuing the integrity of "person" from an indiscriminate *mixture* of

---

6. Plotinus, *Ennead*, 4.7.1.
7. Augustine, *Sermons*, 30.3.4.

different components. However, it is not by demonstration of the inadequacy of a particular construction that major conceptual changes occur, but by working with a new paradigm, thus showing the new paradigm's greater capacity for including and arranging the available evidence. Working with inherited tools, Augustine was unable to propose a new model of person more compatible with Christian faith.

The concluding sentence of my Introduction to *Augustine on the Body* overstates my case: "Augustine was pivotally concerned to integrate his idea of the meaning and value of the body with his philosophical and dogmatic persuasions." True, Augustine saw that the classical model of person needed to be rectified for Christian use, but he could not see how to do it. Lacking a new paradigm, Augustine did not succeed in altering the classical understanding.[8] Throughout his life he continued to praise soul's greater beauty and value at the expense of body, albeit with subtle but significant alterations. In short, Augustine *saw* what he could not *say*. Deep furrows of assumptions and language undermined his effort to name "person" as one entity. Arnold Davidson's eloquent description of the lethargy of mental habits is relevant here—another concept that I did not have until much later. Davidson writes:

> Automisms of attitude have a durability, a slow temporality, which does not match the sometimes rapid change of conceptual mutation. Mental habits have a tendency to inertia, and these habits resist change that, in retrospect, seem conceptually required.[9]

Davidson's description of the struggle of "conceptual mutation" against "mental habits" succinctly articulates Augustine's conspicuous failure to throw the weight of his considerable authority against the strong cultural habit of valuing soul by disparaging body.[10] Nevertheless, the doctrines of Creation, the Incarnation of Jesus Christ, and the resurrection of body played a strong role in Augustine's gradually and partially altered view of

---

8. Augustine discussed even sensation as a foil "demonstrating the grandeur and power of the soul."

9. Davidson, *Emergence of Sexuality*, 91.

10. Similarly, Carol Harrison finds in Augustine's writings "tantalizing hints of a more positive theology of women. against a background largely determined by negative scriptural and social understandings. . . [which] though they contradict his own independent thinking, are unthinkingly reiterated and allowed to influence his work, with no attempt to reconcile, or even articulate, the resulting contradictions." *Augustine, Christian Faith*, 169.

the meaning and value of body. His interest in bodily resurrection focused his strongest statements about human bodies.

> Take away death, the last enemy, and my own flesh shall be my dear friend throughout eternity.[11]
>
> Perfect health of body shall be the ultimate immortality of the whole human.[12]

Augustine on the Body begins to exhibit my growing interest in an historical method that could take into account much more than simply reporting and interpreting what Augustine *said*, the usual method of twentieth-century historical theologians. I wanted to identify the physical, social, and psychological factors that directed and influenced Augustine's intellectual ideas. I read Augustine from the perspective of my own experience of marriages and motherhood, physical pain, and sexual and spiritual longings. My avid reading in the areas of psychology, prompted by the excellent therapy I had received for my ulcer, also informed my understanding of Augustine's experience. In his *Confessions,* Augustine repeatedly described himself as "on fire"—whether in reading Cicero, in his desire to love and be loved, or in reflecting on his experience of God. I too was "inflamed" by my reading. I read voraciously and promiscuously, posting above my desk quotations that encouraged and challenged me.

4

When I wrote *Augustine on the* Body in the mid-1970s, "objectivity" was one of scholarship's highest values. Academics were expected to exclude any mention of heated interest in the subject at hand as well as any life experience. I adopted this detachment, seldom revealing that it was my experience—my particular experience—which led me to consider a text, an idea, or an image beautiful or powerful. Rereading *Augustine on the Body* today, the emotions I felt while writing it, though excluded from the written words, stream back. I relive the fears and excitements of my youth— my anxiety: whether I would get a job, my delight in the privilege of learning and thinking, and my love for the beautiful language of the long-dead Augustine. *Augustine on the Body* is not about me—my own favorite character in fiction—but reading it recalls to me the person I was when I wrote it.

11. Augustine, *Sermons, CLV,* 15.
12. Augustine, *Epistula, CXVIII,* 3.14.

Working with the concepts at hand when writing *Augustine on the Body*, like Augustine I failed to suggest an understanding of "person" that could correct the model I inherited. I merely complained of, and then adopted by default, the longstanding Western intellectual consensus that at best ignored, at worst disparaged body in order to exult in the greater beauty and value of soul. I did not have a more adequate model to suggest. Indeed, an assumption of substantial division stalked my discussion of "being in a body."

Many years later I found a model proposed by the evolutionary biologist, Maxine Sheets-Johnstone, namely the "intelligent body," one entity, not analyzable into distinguishable and competing substances.[13] Sheets-Johnstone describes the "first person" or "intelligent body" as,

> the body that we know directly in the context or process of being alive. It is the body with which we came into the world prior to technology or science telling us what we are made of, how we are put together, how that togetherness works. The body that emerges from the womb alive and kicking is the primordial one. From the moment of birth that body is the center and origin of our being in the world. It is, in fact, our first world and reality. The first-person body is not a body that we outgrow, or even can outgrow; it is only one we can choose to deny or deprecate. It is a body not lacking biological reality, but a body whose biological reality is neither separable from nor a third-person dimension of its lived and living presence.[14]

I needed this model of person from my earliest writings but I did not have it until the 1990s. A more attentive reading of Plato (who is usually accused of introducing "dualism" to Western thought), would have challenged the assumption that human beings, like the universe itself, are composed of components. Plato insisted that the so-called "divided line" between intelligible and sensible worlds does not exist *in reality*, but solely for the purpose of conceptual analysis.[15]

---

13. Miles, *Centaur*, 41.
14. Sheets-Johnstone, *Corporeal Turn*, 20.
15. Plato, *Republic*, VI.509d.

First Publications, 1979 to 1981

Fullness of Life: Historical Foundations for a New Asceticism, 1981

Asceticism is a topic that engaged me from approximately 1981 to 1983, and thereafter as leitmotiv in projects with other foci. In the context of the plethora of consumer goods and entertainment featured in American society, I advocated a mild asceticism based on *choices*. I learned the value of choices in my childhood home. My parents valued "treats"; if we eat ice cream every day, it becomes habitual, and habits are less pleasurable the more they are taken for granted. Augustine, an acute analyzer of pleasure, had a similar objection to self-indulgence. Habits become chains, he said, practices we cannot do without, and bondage is not pleasurable. To discern whether one is "addicted" to a practice or a substance, to see whether a habit has become a chain, try stopping it. If it is difficult or impossible to relinquish—as coffee was for me for several years—it is what Augustine called a "chain"; we call it an addiction.[16]

I experimented with fasting for several years, fasting for three days at a time, drinking only water. During a fast there were moments, perhaps hours at a time, when I had great clarity. *I saw my life*. Or I focused with unusual energy and insight on my studies. The cupboards of my mind opened and thoughts stored in separate compartments played together, yielding understandings to which I had not previously had access. Fasting, I found, has a rhythm; when I felt weak and headachy, I simply rested. But this meant that I could fast only when I had several days free from scheduled activity. As I became busier it became impossible to yield to the rhythm of fasting, so I gave it up. Fasting is not for everyone, or perhaps not for anyone at all times of life. I learned from fasting that ordinary habits of eating and activity protect the intelligent body, hiding its patterns and secrets from consciousness.

I studied historical asceticism, seeking to understand practices, their theological rationale, and their social context. I found that early advocates did not recommend harsh asceticism, counseling instead gentle practices that would simultaneously benefit intelligent bodies. The goal was freedom from distraction and ability to concentrate. By fasting, body was granted what Tertullian called a *vacatione*, a vacation from its constant labor

---

16. "From a perverse will came lust, and slavery to lust became a habit, and a habit, constantly yielded to became a necessity. These were like links, hanging each to each (which is why I call it a chain), and they held me fast in a hard slavery." Augustine, *Confessions*, 8.5.

of digesting food.[17] Both the practices and the rationale of early ascetics seemed appropriate to our own society in which many Americans regularly overindulge in food, drink, entertainment, and consumer goods. In doing so we use far more than our share of the world's resources.

I confess to a certain perverse pleasure in challenging common assumptions—for example, I like to explore words like "asceticism" that we think we understand—and know that we *don't like*. I was partly attracted to studying Augustine *because* he was so universally vilified by modern authors from John Updike to Matthew Fox. In our society, Augustine has a "bad press." Once, after I gave a public lecture on Augustine, someone complained, only partly in jest, "You're making me like a person I want to hate!" I wanted to understand why there was presently such a strong consensus against an author who was highly revered in other times and places.

In *Fullness of Life* I made a young author's common mistake. I thought that if I redefined a word, or indicated that I would be using it in an idiosyncratic way on the first page of an article or book, I could then commence to use it throughout *as I had defined it*—and that readers would understand it throughout in that way. But words are public possessions; common words and concepts are not easily redefined. By the word "asceticism" I wanted to advocate a life-enhancing activity of *choice*. But the word recalled to readers an image of St. Sebastian languishing under a barrage of arrows—or perhaps, the scars of a twenty-first-century self-injurer. In contemporary public usage, the word "asceticism" conveys a virtually unquestioned negative meaning; like Augustine, asceticism has a bad name.

Since it was impossible to place a different meaning and a positive value on "asceticism," I invoked Plan B. I differentiated a so-called "old asceticism" from a "new asceticism." I acknowledged that there is a good deal of "old asceticism" in Christian history— asceticism based on punishing body in the interest of strengthening soul—but there is also "new asceticism," based on gratitude for body, benefit for the whole person, and a desire for "more life."[18] Despite my "solution," the word continued to carry negative associations. I found that advocacy for "asceticism" was counterproduc-

---

17. At that time I accepted the assumption that human persons consisted of "something called mind" (or soul) and "something called body."

18. According to reports from early Christians, Christian faith brought a tremendous surcharge of life: a eucharistic prayer by Serapion of Thmuis (Egypt) prays: "We beg you, make us truly alive." Origen of Alexandria said, "God takes away the deadness in us" (*Comm. In ioannem* 1. 37), and Augustine of Hippo: "Only they can think of God without absurdity who think of him as life itself" (*De doctrina christiana* I.8).

tive.[19] But "choice" is not a perfect synonym for asceticism either; it implies a one-time decision, not an *ongoing daily practice* of thoughtful choosing.

In 1980 when I wrote *Fullness of life*, I did not have the concept of the "intelligent body" that would have enabled a more accurate and nuanced description of asceticism. Even to imagine a "unified" or "whole" person at that time assumed and required the idea of components—the usual suspects, body and soul/mind. The best I could do at the time was the laborious and misleading phrase: "the whole human being, body and soul." Only a model of person that imagines an "intelligent body" can avoid thinking in terms of two (or more) interacting entities, one dominating the other. In *Fullness of Life* and for almost a decade after, I had to be content with demonstrating the centrality of "the body" to Christian life.

"Theology, Anthropology, and the Human Body in Calvin's *Institutes of the Christian Religion*," 1981

This article described the "return of the repressed" body to Calvin's theology. I wanted to show that his understanding of body is central to his understanding of Christian life. Seeking to establish the dependence of theology on anthropology, it carries forward the agenda of my early publications. But my focus on "the body" effectively reified the distinction of body and soul. When I wrote the article I did not know that "the body" (a normative—undoubtedly male—body, lacking specificity and particularity, without sex, ethnicity, social location, age, and other identifying features), *does not exist*. It is an intellectual construct, literally, a figment of the imagination. Calvin desperately needed the "intelligent body" as the foundation for his vision of "the glory of God that fills the universe," creating the "quickening" by which one *sees* "particular events and individual lives as concrete forms of God's glory."

My understanding of Calvin's theology of predestination appears in this article.[20] Luther, who like Calvin (and *un*like Augustine), teaches predestination to reward or damnation—so-called "double predestination"—insisted, in the "Preface" of his *Commentary on Romans*, that the doctrine

---

19. For example, the word "Christian" has been appropriated by media to indicate the Christian Right. A friend who teaches at a Catholic college told me that students frequently told her, "We're not Christians, we're Catholics."

20. I notice that predestination is discussed approvingly only by theologians confident of their election!

can be considered only from a certain perspective, that is, after thoroughly understanding certain doctrinal themes in the book of Romans. Theological intricacies no longer intrigue me as they did when I wrote the article. I leave them to theologians to untangle. Theological abstractions must "collapse into immediacy"[21] before they can affect life and living. I am content and fully engaged every day with Augustine's easy-to-understand, but difficult-to-embody, doctrine of love.

"The Mystical Method of Meister Eckhart," *Studia Mystica*, 1981

The idea that there are moral as well as intellectual requirements for understanding difficult concepts, missing from modern authors, is frequently found in Christian authors of earlier ages. Responding to complaints from his congregation that his preaching was impossible to understand, Eckhart replied that his listeners must meet several moral requirements before they could understand his sermons, challenging the presumption that anyone with intelligence can understand anything adequately articulated. In contemporary parlance "understanding" is thought to mean grasping with the mind, with the mind only; historical authors used the word to indicate grasping with the whole person. Modern thinkers distinguish soul or mind from body to an extreme earlier centuries did not imagine possible. The idea that *living*—how one lives—demonstrates understanding, or failure of understanding, is an historical idea that presently lacks advocates.

In Eckhart's analysis, soul and body do not correspond to inner and outer. "Outer" includes everything resulting from one's birth and socialization—including feelings, "practices," and ritual. The "inner" is the tiniest "kernel" of a person, untouched by social life, where God can be experienced. Eckhart describes an exercise, a *process*, a journey to the core of the soul. The body, storehouse of socialization, must also be "forgotten" on the journey to the kernal. Intellect lies closest to the kernal but it too is external to the inner and must "become as pure ignorance, unknowing (*unwissen*)." Concepts of space, time, and self-consciousness must also be forgotten. In *this* "Now-moment" when the self becomes a perfect void, the birth of God in the soul is consummated. *Now* "Eckhart can speak of the indistinguishability of God and the self."

---

21. R. G. Collingwood's phrase, *The Idea of History*.

Eckhart wrote: "Here the core of God is also my core, and the core of my soul the core of God's." *Now* Eckhart moves to inclusions fully as dramatic as the exclusions he specified at an earlier stage: "our hearts and his are to be one heart; our body and his, one body. So shall it be with our senses, wills, thoughts, faculties, and members: they are all to be transported into him, so that we feel with him and are made aware of him in every part of the body and soul." *Now* self-knowledge *is* knowledge of God. The evidence of God's birth in the soul is the *spontaneity and effortlessness* with which one begins to act virtuously, "without giving it a thought," and "without working at it."

Throughout the history of Christianity the intelligent body has been in the wings, unnamed but necessary in the religion of the Incarnation, but never considered a reality until the anticipated day of resurrection. Meantime, according to Eckhart, body and soul/mind are perennial enemies. The rhetorical usefulness of their distinctness can easily be seen. Even before Christianity, their difference enabled Socrates confidently to expect immortality of soul, a belief mistaken by many to coincide with resurrection of body.[22] Like Augustine, Christian teachers insisted on resurrection of the actual body, *this* body—even speculating that these eyes, *these* very eyes (with which we presently see television), will *see* God. It could not be otherwise in the religion of the "Word made flesh."

"The Courage to be Alone—In and Out of Marriage," *The Feminist Mystic*, 1982

I would now title this article, "The Courage to be By Myself..." The difference is critical. Hannah Arendt wrote: "When Socrates goes home, he is not alone, he is *by himself*."[23] The word "alone" implies an absence, an empty place filled with longing, a lack. "By himself," on the other hand suggests a self-relationship that is filled with one's life, rich with memories alive in the present, with reflection and pleasurable dialogue within oneself.

At the time the article was written, however, I was not "by myself"; I was "alone." I had moved across the continent from Berkeley, California, to Cambridge, Massachusetts, "alone," facing new challenges, new

---

22. Christian belief is that the intelligent body—the person—is resurrected; immortality of the soul states that at the death of body, soul goes on living, detaching from the dead and biodegradable body.

23. Arendt, *Thinking*, 187.

experiences. The article summarizes the ideas and images I found with which to construct courage. "Staying is nowhere," Rilke wrote, and I often repeated to myself. The way to know myself, I thought, was to place myself in different circumstances, different environments, and observe how I act.

A sentence from Arthur Miller's play "The Misfits" articulated my experience in two failed marriages. In the movie version, the Marilyn Monroe character, having established the required residency in Nevada, is climbing the long steps to the courthouse to finalize her divorce. Her estranged husband, endeavoring to stop the proceedings, appears suddenly and urges her not to divorce him. She replies, "If I'm going to be alone I want to be by myself." I realized that I must transform being alone into being "by myself." Aloneness is a reality: we are born and we die alone; "by myself" is a choice.

Reading my early publications I see that I had ideas that are still timely for me thirty-five years ago. My life seems to have been a long saga of understanding, forgetting, rediscovering, and relearning. The concept of "relationship" is an example: relationship is usually understood as requiring two entities, two persons who agree to build a bridge across the chasm between them. An alternative interpretation of that idea of relationship is *exploring a connection*, a connectedness. This idea of relationship is helpful whether the "other" is God or another person. I knew this intellectually in 1982; I am still in process of weaving it into my life.

Chapter 3

Tenure, 1982 to 1985

1

IN A NARRATIVE ACCOUNT, the movement from entrance-level professor to tenure sounds smooth and swift. A few pages after arriving at Harvard, I have tenure. In life, it was not so. Recall Luther's admonition to remember that the outcome was unknown to the protagonist! My years as a junior professor seemed at once to proceed very rapidly, providing little time to publish articles and books to prepare for promotion deliberations, *and* very slowly. Seven years was a long time to *not know* whether I had a future at Harvard Divinity School. Compound that realistic uneasiness with the knowledge that at that time Harvard had a poor record of granting tenure to junior faculty. In fact, no junior faculty, male or female, had received tenure at HDS in the preceding twenty years. And no woman had received tenure since the school's origin as a graduate faculty of Harvard University in 1816. The odds were not favorable.[1]

It seemed wise for my new husband and me to develop a Plan B. Owen, approaching the last few years of a long career at the Episcopal Divinity School in Cambridge, agreed that if I did not receive tenure he would move with me to wherever I found employment. If I was given tenure, I agreed to stay with him in Cambridge so that he could complete his career at EDS. To spare my friends, I paid a therapist to listen to my repetitive anxieties.

1. Tenure proceedings at HDS have changed in several ways since 1985.

Tenure proceedings included a search for "the best in the world" in my field—junior faculty called it the "intergalactic search." In short, the process was not only a matter of considering the quality and quantity of my work, but of comparing it to the work of others in my field. When tenure deliberations began, there was nothing I could do to encourage a generous consideration of my publications and classroom evaluations, so I tried to ignore the situation, even when candidates for "my" position gave interview lectures down the hall from my classroom." As my junior appointment came to a close, and the decision regarding promotion to tenure loomed, I endeavored to focus on the *pleasure* of teaching and writing rather than the fear that I could shortly be without a job.

After considering all the candidates, the tenured faculty of divinity would vote on whether or not to forward to the president of Harvard University a recommendation for my promotion. If the recommendation was favorable, the president would appoint an *ad hoc* committee of scholars outside the university to evaluate my publications and advise him on the promotion. He would then make the decision; I was granted tenure in May 1985.

2

As a junior professor I found a way to make teaching and publishing work together. "History of Christian Thought" lectures provided research and ideas for articles. Each time the course was offered I researched historical authors more deeply. Articles on Augustine, Luther, Calvin, and Eckhart were my first publications after my dissertation, *Augustine on the Body*. Seminars gave me opportunity to lay the groundwork for books. Seminars focused on the subjects and authors I needed to explore in depth; students read translations, and I consulted original texts on points central to the author's argument. In the next term after a semester, I offered a lecture course on the subject; my detailed lecture notes, informed by the earlier seminar's critical reading, could then be "written up" quite quickly (in a summer) as chapters in a book.

Perhaps others had already learned this method of coordinating teaching and publishing. I learned it "on location." I could not have managed if I had thought of teaching and writing as two *separate* endeavors competing for my time. It seemed to me that the fruit of research, thinking, and writing should enhance the classroom; lectures and seminar discussions offered a perfect arena in which to benefit from students' responses—critical and appreciative—to both the texts we read together and my interpretations. By making teaching and writing for publication *work together*, I was able to publish both sufficiently and with a quality commensurate with a positive tenure decision.

3

"Infancy, Parenting, and Nourishment in Augustine's *Confessions*," *Journal of the American Academy of Religion*, 1982

Augustine's *Confessions* describes *concupiscentia* as anxious grasping at everything that crosses one's path in the fear that something will be missed. In Augustine's usage, *concupiscentia* did not refer only—or even primarily—to sexual acquisitiveness.[2] It also included lust for power and lust for possessions. In this article I should have explained further the connection between these three lusts; what they have in common is that they are each strong enough to subvert and redirect a person's goals and energies. Although as a young man, Augustine's primary compulsion was sex, he gives examples of the "red hot" jealousies[3] that revealed his ancillary lusts for power and possessions.

Augustine said that the appropriate reaction to *concupiscentia* is sympathy for the person suffering from it—yes, suffering.[4] Surprisingly, Augustine thought that *concupiscentia* occurs at its greatest intensity in infants. The first involuntary act of a neonate is to gasp/grasp breath, a concupiscent action that is the paradigm and origin of future grasping. Moreover, the infant does not trust that anyone will care for, feed, or notice it unless s/he demands it. As children grow, the objects of *concupiscentia* change, but not the basic fear response that something intimately and vitally important will be missed.[5]

2. Bonner, "*Libido* and *Concupiscentia*."
3. Augustine, *Confessions*, 3.1.
4. Augustine, *Confessions*, 1.9.
5. Augustine, *Confessions*, 1.19; Augustine says that as the child grows to adulthood, objects of *concupiscentia* change from "footballs, nuts, and pet sparrows [to] gold, estates, and slaves."

The word "anxiety" that I used throughout the article to name the origin of *concupiscence* is imprecise. *Concupiscence* is prompted by *fear,* the fear that something—*life*—will be missed. Fear is a stronger, more active, more specific, emotion than anxiety, an aggressive compelling force. Anxiety can equally indicate catatonic passivity. Fear is also the *opposing* power that prevents love. Fear drains the psyche's strength and energy, leaving nothing with which to *make* love.

First John 4:18 was a favorite passage of Augustine's: "Perfect love casts out fear." To the extent that the psyche is governed by fear, love has no "weight" (*pondeus*). Augustine wrote: "In proportion as the dominion of *concupiscence* is dismantled, in the same proportion, love is built up."[6] Augustine returns to the image of the infant at the breast to describe the substitution of grateful acceptance for aggressive demand: "What am I, at my best, but an infant suckling the milk you give and feeding upon you, the food that is imperishable?"[7]

4

There are few academic rewards beyond the considerable luxury of a life in thought. My colleagues and I often observed, "If you do a good job, you don't get money and a vacation; you get *more work.*" But a month-long fellowship at the Rockefeller Study and Conference Center in Bellagio, Italy, is a rare and lavish academic reward. In 1983 I was granted a fellowship at the Rockefeller Center. My husband, Owen Thomas, and I arrived at the Villa Serbelloni to find a sign on our door, "Mr. and Mrs. Thomas." My husband's name has never been my name; when we married I did not change my name because by then I had publications in my maiden name. Since the appointment was mine, his name on the door annoyed me. I asked that the sign be replaced with "Margaret Miles and Owen Thomas." The managers tried again: "Mr. and Mrs. Miles." They explained that the point that we were married had to be made; "partners" were not acceptable at the Rockefeller Center in 1982. Finally, on our insistence, the sign was corrected. Shortly after, the policy was changed; "significant others" and "life partners" were welcomed at the Rockefeller Center. When we returned in 1993—Owen's appointment this time—there was no problem!

---

6. Augustine, *De doctrina christiana*, 3.10.
7. Augustine, *Confessions*, 4.1.

Tenure, 1982 to 1985

Each Fellow gave an informal talk on the subject of her/his proposal. But the most stimulating conversations occurred at breakfast, lunch, and dinner—all wonderful Italian meals. Drinks before both lunch and dinner aided the conversation! At dinner, place cards guaranteed that we circulated among the fifteen or twenty fellows and their spouses in the course of the month.

Each of us had a studio. Mine was a lovely little house in the woods, a perfect place to work. If we chose not to return to the villa for lunch we could ask for a bag lunch to be eaten in our studio. I expected to find that a luxurious life such as this did not produce good writing, but in my case, it did. In order to get the most from the month of work, leisure, and luxury, a writing project should be at the revising stage, not the research stage, as the villa did not have an adequate research library for the many projects to be worked on there. My project at the Rockefeller Center was my "tenure book," *Image as Insight*, the book that would be examined by colleagues at Harvard and other institutions in process of a tenure recommendation.

Working styles differed greatly among the fellows. One rose early in the morning, ran, and then wrote with concentration until mid-afternoon when he took boat trips around the lake until dinner. Every day. Another Fellow was always drunk, stoned, or both. Crumbs surrounded his plate at meals as he had difficulty finding his mouth with the fork. *Both were excellent writers.* I admired the second fellow's wife, who seemed to feel no chagrin over her husband's behavior. She ignored him and enjoyed new friends, silk shopping in Como, and excursions around the lake.

Artists, novelists, film critics, poets, and musicians also received appointments at the Rockefeller Study and Conference Center, making for a diverse and lively group. The "fellow pilgrims" were a large part of the treat. But the greatest pleasure was the exquisitely beautiful natural surroundings. The villa is on a hill above Lake Como, beyond which one can see Switzerland. My Bellagio experience was an immensely rich privilege, one for which I am very grateful. I think that Owen and I are one of few couples who enjoyed *two* months at Bellagio, each of us receiving a one-month appointment a decade apart.

"Vision: The Eye of the Body and the Eye of the Mind in St. Augustine's *De Trinitate* and the *Confessions*," *The Journal of Religion*, 1983

The title of this article reveals my adoption of the inherited model of "person" as stacked components, usually soul/mind and body. In *De trinitate*, Augustine suggests that the "eye of the mind" relies on the "eye of the body." He struggled to describe an experience in which "the two together are one." He needed the "intelligent body"! Vision, queen of the senses, was considered the appropriate metaphor for understanding: I *see*. Lacking a concept of the intelligent body, I understated Augustine's identification of spiritual vision *with* physical vision. I said, "Augustine extrapolates a nuanced account of spiritual vision from his model of physical vision." I did not quite say that Augustine actually suggested that physical vision *could be* spiritual vision.

Unlike hearing, in which a sound of a certain loudness is passively heard by any hearing person, vision requires not only divine illumination but also human effort, according to Augustine. Human effort includes the choice of an object on which to focus, concentration, and cleansing the eye of the mind "whereby God can be seen." Modern accounts of vision emphasize the *distance* between seer and seen; Augustine, however, accepted Plato's model of vision, which emphasized the *connection* of seer and object.[8] Plato taught that vision occurs when a ray of light, projected from the eye, *touches* its object; rays "shine through the eyes and touch whatever we see."[9] Moreover, the visual ray is a two-way street: the object seen moves back up the visual ray and is printed on the viewer's memory.

The ancient account of physical vision with which Augustine worked has long been replaced by scientific accounts of the mechanics of vision. But as a description of religious vision it remains accurate. It assumes a *dialogue* between a spiritual object and a person in which *both contribute*. In Augustine's understanding, the soul contributes the energy of longing

---

8. Augustine described two mystical experiences in his *Confessions*. In 7.17 he used the metaphor of vision to describe the apex of the experience: "And then in the flash of a trembling glance, my mind arrived at That Which Is." In *Confessions* 9.10, he described the apex of his experience with his mother, Monnica, as transcending vision: "And as we talked, yearning toward this Wisdom, we did, with the whole strength of our hearts' impulse, just lightly come into *touch* with her (Wisdom)."

9 Augustine, *De trinitate*, 9.3.3.

and the cleansed and exercised visual ray; the object's contribution is soul-shaping truth.

Augustine's description of vision is deeply informed by the scripture verse he quoted more frequently than any other in his long career as a preacher and writer, 1 Corinthians 13:23, "We see now through a glass darkly, then, however, face to face."[10] Now (*nunc*) the glimpse; then (*tunc*) the gaze. The training of the eye of the mind for the vision of God *is* the activity of loving.

The themes developed in this article became the themes of both my scholarly and my personal interest: vision, longing, seeing the "world of the eyeball"—as Plato put it[11]—with a loving eye, the eye that sees God in the "neighbor," the natural world, and every beauty.

"The Pursuit of Lifefulness: In Search of a Method," *Studia Mystica*, 1984

"We beg you, make us truly alive." The fourth-century eucharistic prayer, attributed to Serapion of Thmuis (in Egypt), articulates a major theme of early Christian writings, namely, that Christian faith conquered deadness, bringing life to the believer. Augustine wrote: "Anyone who thinks of God as anything other than Life Itself has an absurd idea of God."[12] This article reviews the film, "My Dinner with André," a late twentieth-century secular exploration of how to get and keep a vivid sense of life.

André, a playwright, describes to Wally, a struggling actor, the wild adventures by which he sought "more life." Wally, who declares himself content with an ordinary life, is happy if he does not find a dead cockroach floating in his cup of cold coffee in the morning. André and Wally agreed that the deadness of everyday life is caused by comfort and habits, but their proposals for overcoming deadness differ. Wally advocates lowered expectations, acceptance of ordinary life, and enjoyment of small pleasures: "I don't think I feel the need for anything more." André advocated more extreme measures, including withdrawal from the familiar, "taking to the road." Wild parties in Poland and experiments simulating death and challenging André's comfort zone created his feeling of aliveness.

---

10. *Videmus nunc per speculum in aenigmate; tunc autem, facie ad faciem.*
11. Plato, *Republic*, VI.509d
12. Augustine, *De doctrina christiana*, 1.8.

Considering both proposals, I advocated gentle asceticism, as good for body as for soul, as a way to address habits and addictions. My experiments with short fasts, abstinence from coffee, and altering habitual behaviors had revealed the capacity of small changes to produce "more life."[13]

The longing to be fully alive continues to be a dominant theme of my life and my work,[14] though ascetic practices belong to an earlier time in my life. I resemble Wally more than André. I like my life; I work, and I love the people I'm with, Freud's criteria for psychic health. The fourth-century ascetics of the Egyptian desert used their prayer lives as a criterion of health: if their prayer life was blocked, they designed an ascetic practice to address the problem. Ability to love and work are the modern secular equivalent for mental health.

"Voyeurism and Visual Images of Violence," *The Christian Century*, 1984

In this article I compared the effects of visual images of violence in the television film "The Day After" with the violent images of Mathias Grünewald's "Isenheim Altarpiece." "The Day After" was *intended* to generate protest against the stockpiling of nuclear weapons. I suggested that it failed to do so.

Visual associations inform and direct viewers' reactions to violent images. I argued that violent images viewers can relate to only voyeuristically do not arouse them to protest the depicted violence. Viewers, accustomed to media depictions of violence as entertainment, are merely entertained. Momentarily titillated, we quickly forget the suffering.

By contrast, the Isenheim Altarpiece, its purpose and its location, addressed suffering directly. Located in a hospital monastery, patients suffering from the contemporary illness displayed in the wounds of the suffering Christ were regularly brought to view the painting. The painting told them that Christ shared their suffering, and encouraged them to pray for healing

---

13. The traditional model of "person" as stacked components explains the dynamics of asceticism based on the "unity" of human being: "Whatever affects the body affects the soul." But "unity" requires two (or more) entities, brought together. It does not explain how entities of different *substances,* as body and soul are imagined to be within this model, can affect one another. Once again I needed, and did not have, the "intelligent body."

14. In fact, "the two together are one." I never conceptualized academic work and personal life as separate entities. Personal life and academic work were deeply consanguineous.

and/or endurance. The altarpiece was expected to produce real effects in the lives of its viewers.

I began to recognize an activity in which thinking and feeling are "coordinated." Not yet interwoven, indistinguishable, and still emerging from different components of the self, I began to understand that "they" are one activity. But, how to say *one* activity? We *do* it all the time; we think feelingly and we feel thoughtfully, but how to *say* it?[15]

"'The Rope Breaks When it Is Tightest': Luther on the Body, Consciousness, and the Word," *Harvard Theological Review*, 1984

Luther (an Augustinian monk) was "preoccupied with the heavy undertow of his recalcitrant body"; he thought of his body as *other than,* but a mirror of his "wildly aroused and disturbed conscience."[16] As if he used Augustine's narrative of conversion (described in book 8 of his *Confessions*) as a template, Luther foreshortened and dramatized his conversion in the telling. As with Augustine, sudden understanding was prompted by a scriptural passage. Luther had previously understood the passage intellectually; he had even lectured on it at the University of Wittenberg. Now he understood it "at the bottom of the heart." Words, "the just shall live by faith," became for him "the Word of God," a key to all scripture, and a "real gate to paradise."

By contrast with the leisurely complexity of late medieval theologians (such as Duns Scotus and William of Ockham), Luther's theology is simple, revolving around a few points. As discussed in the Preface to this book, Luther believed that God hears the sinner's plea for rescue *only* when it is prompted by abject terror. His paradigm was Jonah in the belly of the great fish.

Sixteenth-century catechisms for children exemplify Lutheran attempts to bring children to the overpowering consciousness of utter helplessness that prompts a cry for salvation. Luther did not himself write children's catechisms, but they are faithful renderings of his theology. Children were expected to memorize these catechisms from as early an age as possible. They contain long lists of evildoings to which the child must confess saying, we are "killers, whoremongers, idol worshippers, miscreants, adulterers, thieves and rogues"—a partial list. Penalties were also to

15. Recall Sheets-Johnstone, "There is no 'they.'"
16. Quotations are from the article discussed.

be memorized: "fever, swellings, pestilence, sores and boils, and altogether so much terror, misery, [and] suffering... that [the child] must fall into despair."[17] However, precisely at the point of utter despair and hopelessness, catechisms suddenly shift to "strong and moving assurances of God's love and forgiveness for the 'miserable offenders.'" Catechisms skillfully recreate the psychology of Luther's theology in which the child is brought to utmost despair, then swiftly reassured of God's mercy.

I try to imagine the perspective from which these children's catechisms seemed to sixteenth-century Lutherans to be skillful tools for the Christian life. Clearly, my own religious sensibility is an inadequate tool, resulting only in judgment—a dead giveaway that I have not understood![18]

Image as Insight: Visual Understanding in Western Christianity and Secular Culture, 1985

> The Word is no other than see.[19]
>
> By use of the bodily eyes everyone possesses all that he delights to see.[20]
>
> We are answerable for what we learn how to see.[21]
>
> What one loves and desires depends upon how one sees.[22]

In 1984 I was granted a Presidential Leave to prepare for my tenure review. Owen also had a sabbatical year, and we spent that year in Rome and Bellagio, Italy. During that year I wrote a different book than the book I was planning to offer for my review; libraries in Rome were unfamiliar and difficult. I was not allowed to enter one library because it was in a monastery and women were not allowed. I worked mainly at the Herziana, the art history library above the Spanish steps; sometimes I worked at the Vatican

---

17. For further discussion of Lutheran catechisms for children, see my *Word Made Flesh*, 253–54.

18. It is necessary to imagine a monumental shift of values. I am somewhat helped in this exercise by recalling my fundamentalist father's perspective: he honestly thought that leaving a young waitress a tract outlining the way of salvation was a far greater gift than leaving a tip.

19. Jan van Ruysbroech.

20. Augustine, *De trinitate* 14.19.

21. Haraway, "Persistence of Vision," 285.

22. Astell, *Eating Beauty*, 135.

library. At these libraries scholars were not allowed to browse in the stacks. Each morning I sent in a request for the books I needed. Thirty or forty minutes later an attendant would deliver the books. The library closed at 1:00 p.m., reopening at 4:00. I was told that Romans went home, ate a large lunch, undressed, and took a nap. Then they got up and started their day all over again. The day ended with dinner at 10:00 p.m.

This was not the way I was accustomed to working. At home in the United States I was accustomed to working early in the day; I often got up at 5:00 a.m. and wrote for two or three hours before going to my office. But this schedule required an early bedtime. I understood why graduate students working on their dissertations in Italy take a long time to finish! At first I thought the Roman hours of working and leisure demonstrated that graduate students were not *serious* about their work. By the end of my time in Italy I realized that graduate students working in Italy were healthier than many American graduate students who worked all day, crawling out of the library, blinking, at closing time.

I dedicated my tenure book, *Image as Insight,* to my husband, Owen Thomas, the first man I had been with who was not jealous of my work; he *let me work*! Sometimes he appeared at my door carrying an armload of books from his own library that he thought would be useful for my next lecture. He even brought *his* work and worked while I worked! This was quite unprecedented in my experience, and amazing to me. I had thought that if I was to be able to do my work, I would need to be single. I married Owen in 1981.

Image as Insight was the first book in which I specified a political agenda. The Preface explains that to understand the symbolic resources of *most* historical people it is not sufficient to rely on writings of a few (almost inevitably male) educated, privileged, and authoritative leaders. The history of people who do not rely on language to define their reality cannot be reconstructed from the linguistically-trained men of the past. The visual images of Western Christianity—the democratic media of the past—were in parish churches that, together with scripture and sermons, constituted the religious repertoire of largely illiterate medieval Christian communities for understanding themselves, their societies, and the world.

I struggled to describe the need of the "whole human being" for both language and images, identifying "subjective consciousness" with "the life of the mind," and images with "the life of the body." Wrong again! I could not imagine the intelligent body; you can't get there from here! Chapter two in *Image as Insight*, "Hermeneutics and the History of Image Users," is a rather complex defense of the use of images as historical evidence. I argue that *both* language and images present the possibility of multiple interpretations in different cultural, social, and physical locations. Language cannot be privileged for its greater precision and clarity. Chapters 3, 4, and 5 give several examples of the value of images for reconstructing the symbolic resources of Christian communities: fourth-century Christian Rome, fourteenth-century Tuscany, and sixteenth-century Protestant and Roman Catholic reformations. Two final chapters bring my analysis to the present, discussing contemporary media—news photographs and advertisements—and offering a theory of images as historical evidence.

Language, from Socrates forward, was considered a therapeutic tool for correcting "misrepresentations of reality" reflecting conceptual and perceptual disorientation. In Plato's dialogues, Socrates and his friends examine commonly misunderstood words like "courage" and "beauty." Rather than arguing to an incontestable definition, Socrates was content to *discuss* concepts from a number of different perspectives, not seeking to arrive at a irrefutable conclusion. For example, after discussing the question, What is beauty? Plato concluded his only treatise on beauty: "All that is beautiful is difficult."[23]

Perhaps unsurprisingly, I declared that *historians* should teach and write about philosophers. When a philosopher expounds the concepts of an historic author, he is likely to trace the long development of the author's ideas—usually from Plato forward—apparently assuming that ideas have a life of their own, that they drop from the clouds unaffected by the particularities of circumstances. A historian assumes, rather, that ideas emerge from lives; individuals and communities find a concept valuable because it articulates or clarifies contemporary personal or social conversations, problems, or experiences. Historians consider the author's education, social location and circumstances, conversation partners, and other variables as evidence permits. The historian also knows that the author must have been esteemed by his society since his writings are preserved. For example, women's writings are rare, not only because most women did not have education and/or leisure in which to write, but also because their writings were not valued and thus were not preserved.

In *Image as Insight* I proposed that language and images are complementary. Images *attract* viewers to imitation of the religious, social, and

---

23. Plato, *Greater Hippias*, 304e.

personal values depicted in the image.²⁴ Language articulates those values and critiques them, articulating the image's communication *within the symbolic repertoire of its society of origin*. The image's audience can also be identified. I urged readers to construct a *repertoire* of images that address one's needs in different times of life, on different days or moments. Images can not only *remind* us of a value; they can also bring us *to* that value.²⁵

Language, especially poetic language, can heal. Intelligent bodies need both attraction and critical analysis—systole and diastole—exercised and refined over a lifetime. Moreover, I may actively engage with a painting, a piece of music, or a poem for a long time before I am able to articulate with precision why it attracts me. Finally I must discern whether it is useful *for me in that moment* of my life. Do I need, in that moment, resigned acceptance or engagement, rest or energy for a struggle that needs my support?

---

24. Michel Foucault differentiated "strong power," the power to attract, from "weak power," coercion, which becomes necessary only when power to attract (to the values and practices of an institution or society) is no longer effective.

25. To illustrate: at the death of a loved one I found both a focus and relief in externalizing and objectifying my grief. Giotto's "Crucifixion" at the Scrovegni Chapel, Padua, served well. The hysterical grief of the angels darting above the cross, together with the figures of St. John, the Virgin, and Mary Magdalen huddled in catatonic grief at the foot of the cross *acted out* for me the embodiments of grief. Similarly, I found an objectification for grief for my son's narrow escape from death in Heinrich Schütz's "Fili mi Absalon"—a musical composition in which King David laments the death of his son, Absalon.

PART II

Chapter 4

Teaching and Writing, 1986 to 1996

> People know what they do; they frequently know why they do what they do; but what they don't know is what what they do *does*.[1]

FREED FROM ANXIETY ABOUT whether I would be awarded tenure, I found a new ease and passion in writing. I began to develop what I called "the queer eye," the eye that looks at evidence from a different (than traditional) slant, asking different (than traditional) questions that enabled me to understand in different ways. To illustrate: traditional church historians assumed that the "winning" interpretation (as approved by an ecumenical council) is the "right" interpretation. A teaching fellow who lectured on the fourth-century Christological controversies in my History of Christian Thought course reveals this assumption. He asked, "Where did Arius go wrong?" By contrast, the "queer eye" historian asks instead, what were the assumptions, values, and loyalties of each of the interpretations? What did Arius—and others whose positions "lost" at the council in which they were voted—highlight and respect? The following article asked "queer eye" questions of the Christian alternatives in fourth-century Roman North Africa.

---

1. Foucault, quoted in Dreyfus and Rabinow, *Michel Foucault*, 187.

RECOLLECTIONS AND RECONSIDERATIONS

"Roman North African Christian Spiritualties," *African Spirituality: Forms, Meanings, and Expressions*," Jacob Olupona, ed., 2000

History is always the history of the present. Contemporary Christianity is better served by a history of diversity than a triumphal history that pictures the incremental development of an orthodox consensus, together with the exclusion of "heretical" dissidents. In the "development" thesis, Roman Christianity, the historic "winner," was the only adequate expression of Christianity. In this article I wanted to place the several most populated forms of North African Christianity on a conceptual "level playing field," discussing the loyalties, insights, and values of each; I sought to examine the differing interpretations of Christianity in Roman North Africa from an ecumenical perspective. In doing so I found that each of the veins in the North African Body of Christ was committed to emphasizing and carrying forward strongly rooted North African Christian values.[2]

Augustine was at the center of fourth- and fifth-century theological conflicts in North Africa. He was *both* a "native son," *and* one who had experienced the Catholic Church outside North Africa. His allegiance to the "catholic" Roman church made the unity—construed as unanimity of belief—of the "worldwide" (meaning empire-wide) Church his highest priority. He defended Roman doctrine (as he understood and interpreted it), but he also described the church as a *corpus permixtus*, an untidy pile of "wheat and tares," lying promiscuously on the threshing floor until judgment day. *Doctrinal* unity allowed him to accept an unfiltered crowd of sinners rubbing shoulders in the church.

> One who enters is bound to see drunkards, misers, tricksters, gamblers, adulterers, fornicators, people wearing amulets, clients of sorcerers, astrologers . . . the same crowds who press into the churches on Christian festivals also fill the theaters on pagan holidays.[3]

---

2. The article was written in 1986; it was not published until 2000. The delay in publication left me in an awkward position as my article did not take into account the most recent work on Christian movements in Roman North Africa, for example, Maureen Tilley's important work on Donatism. By the time the book went into production I was engaged with other projects and had no time for extensive revisions.

3. Augustine, *De catechizandis rudibus*, 25.48.

Augustine, intransigent on matters of doctrine, was surprisingly tolerant in matters of practice.[4] Donatists valued *purity*, defined as a church uncorrupted by clergy who allegedly had handed over the scriptures to Roman authorities in earlier times of persecution.

Other Christian groups discussed in the essay are Manichaeans and Montanists. North African values were also evident in these groups. Montanists championed leadership by the Holy Spirit over that of bishops and clergy. But the Spirit's leadership might be evidenced in unexpected "vessels," such as women and/or confessors. It threatened ordained clergy, and thus was hotly contested by bishops like Cyprian. Recalling the times of persecution and martyrdom, Manichaeans' theology and practices focused on sensitivity to suffering, from plants and animals to human beings.[5]

Placing North African Christian movements on a *conceptual* "level playing field" however does nothing to equalize the religious and social *power* of the various groups. Augustine confessed that he changed his mind from initially believing that no one should be coerced to communion with the Roman Church.[6] He explained that he had become convinced that "compelling them to enter" was right because several Donatists had told him that coercion had brought them to understand and embrace catholic Christianity. It was power, not conviction, which carried the day in North Africa.

"The Virgin's One Bare Breast: Female Nudity and Religious Meaning in Tuscan Early Renaissance Culture," *The Female Body in Western Culture*, 1986

This article became a base for my future work. It was my first publication that was prompted by visual evidence. I was startled to notice, in many late medieval and renaissance paintings, the Virgin Mary with one breast exposed, usually offering it to the infant Jesus. In its society-of-origin, the image was heavy with theological and social meaning.

Extensive historical research is necessary if one seeks to determine the meaning or meanings a subject carried within its society of origin. An historical image cannot be understood from the perspective and visual

---

4. For example, he permitted Christians baptized in the Donatist Church to enter the catholic Church without rebaptism.

5. See Miles, "Jesus patabilis," 3–18.

6. Augustine, *Epistula*, 185.

training of a person in a very different social setting. What were the visual associations the original viewers of these paintings were "likely to have had" with an image of an exposed breast?[7] Research into the emotional, theological, social, and physical issues surrounding nourishment in fourteenth-century Tuscany at the time the paintings were commissioned brought to light some complex religious and social reasons for viewers' interest.

An historian usually expects that written evidence will help to interpret the visual evidence of a society's internal, and often it does. But there are other possibilities. Verbal evidence can also be indifferent to visual; it can come from a different—even antagonistic—social or institutional location within the same society. Moreover, jarring dissonance between the church authorities' (who commissioned paintings, stipulating in detail theme and treatment) *intended* message, and the "messages likely received" complicate the interpretation. In the case of images of the Virgin with an exposed breast, I discovered that the "messages intended" and the "messages received" were richly—bewilderingly—abundant. They revealed a vivid anxiety surrounding nourishment in fourteenth-century Tuscan society. The article required an increment of sophistication in my approach to historical images. I was not finished with the Virgin's bare breast!

"Introduction," *Immaculate and Powerful: The Female in Sacred Image and Social Reality*, 1987

This edited volume emerged from the Harvard Women's Studies in Religion program. My introduction named several themes that arose in essays from different disciplines in the Study of Religion—biblical studies, Hindu and Tibetan studies, African American studies, and nineteenth and twentieth-century studies.

A motif running through the essays is the ambiguity in women's lives of male-designed and administered religion. Religion can both oppress and authorize women. Our authors agreed that whether one or the other dominates in women's lives depends on how women use religious resources. Essays examine the creativity with which some women have been able to

---

7. Not "must have had," but a less assertive locution based on documentation. After being scolded in a review of *Image as Insight* in the *New York Times Book Review* for writing "would have," I adopted the more careful phrase. Historians, I now think, can say anything they think they see in their evidence *as long as* they acknowledge with precision what the evidence permits—from "I speculate" to more confident assertions based on documentation.

choose among the many messages they receive from their religion, appropriating those that enable and strengthen them, and rejecting those that are limiting. The interaction of religion and culture is also critical. Does religion effectively challenge the secular culture in which it exists? Does it offer alternatives to secular values? Or does it lend its authority to reinforcing oppressive values?

Deploring the paucity of stories and images of strong women in Western cultures, Western feminists often imagine that such images would necessarily lead to remedied gender assumptions and social arrangements. This assumption is inaccurate. Our essays suggest that there is often a disconnect between symbols and social arrangements. For instance, Hindu societies, in which strong images of women are abundant and accessible, still maintain male dominance.

Feminist scholars read texts of the cultures we study differently than we learned in graduate school. We tend to read male-authored texts, not for what the author is trying to communicate, but for what they *reveal* about the author's gender assumptions. Also, in texts written by men, the success of male control of women often acts as a measure of the health and viability of a society.

"Violence Against Women in the Historical Christian West and in North American Secular Culture: The Visual and Textual Evidence," *Shaping New Vision: Gender and Values in American Culture*, 1987

The astoundingly high figures for rape and other violence against women in the United States (in 1986 when the essay was written) suggest that violence against women is well supported from myriad points within American society. Studies of societies in which rape is absent or rare demonstrate that rape is not "simply a biological fact of life," the result of rampant male hormones.[8] It occurs, rather, in societies in which public culture suggests and supports violence against women. What images and ideas support the high level of violence against women in Western cultures? The essay examines Jewish and Christian "contributions" to a symbolic repertoire that fosters violence against women.

---

8. Sanday, *Female Power and Male Dominance*.

Recollections and Reconsiderations

My understanding of feminist historiography was not in place by 1986. Later I was told that in 1977, when I was being considered for an appointment at HDS, graduate student women worried about my credentials as a feminist. They consulted with a student colleague at the Graduate Theological Union where I did my doctoral studies. To this day I do not know whether she told them that I was completely innocent of any acquaintance with feminism or whether, after talking with me, she told them that I was a fast learner! Thus I never knew whether I was hired *because* I could be expected to be (at least) favorable to the study of feminism (satisfying women students), or whether I was hired for my lack of knowledge of feminism (pleasing male colleagues).

I *was* a fast learner and, largely under the tutelage of women students at Harvard Divinity School, I rapidly read myself into the conversation. The Women's Studies in Religion Resource Associates Program at HDS was an important influence. The program brought five Women's Studies scholars in various fields to the school every year to teach one course, pursue their own research, and give a public lecture. Feminist ideas and methods infiltrated HDS through this program. The scholars who came to HDS were learned and generous conversation partners. HDS is indebted to this program for the challenge and excitement it brought to traditional fields. When I arrived at HDS in 1978, feminism was "in the air."

I was startled and outraged when I *noticed* the treatment of women in historical and contemporary societies. Since then I have frequently noticed in others—students and colleagues—a similar angry reaction when they identify with women "as a caste," as Mary Daly put it. When one does this it is no longer possible to set oneself outside of, and untouched by, the marginalization and oppression of women. However, this emotional reaction, though warranted, is only the impetus for the scholarship and activism needed not only to notice, but also to change, women's lives and the range of their opportunities.

I struggled with how to work with feminist perspectives in the classroom. In the late 1980s feminists were divided by strong opinions as to whether women needed women-only institutional space in which to confer on matters relating to feminist values and agenda, or whether feminism should be "mainstreamed," woven into what counted as knowledge in all academic fields. I chose the mainstream approach, including attention to women throughout my courses. I thought that until Women's Studies became an integral part of "history" (as well as other fields) men, as well as most women, would not be persuaded of its centrality and necessity.[9] I hoped that becoming accustomed to noticing the lives and interests of historical women in my classes might prompt students to *miss* and ask for attention to women in other courses.

My essays in the books published by the Women's Studies in Religion program were my first effort to place my voice among feminist scholars. "Violence against Women" clearly participates in my outrage at the multiple religious texts and images that *have been used* and *can be used* to support, to authorize and encourage violence against women. From the "playful" sexism of everyday life, well known to women, to contemporary news stories of women stoned to death in the Middle East, women are targets for men's "fun," frustration, and deadly anger.

Does scholarship produce change? Feminist activists sometimes scorn scholars whose work exposes sexism in texts and images, in institutions, in relationships and social arrangements. Yet scholarship supports activism, calling attention and seeking change. In fact, scholarship itself *is* activism. The Women's Movement suffers when hierarchies of relative importance are created. *All* are needed to do what each does best in support of the major social change that is happening in our day.

In my feminist essays I did not advocate what I did not yet understand, namely that historians must develop a complex hermeneutics that is *both* sympathetic and critical. For a time my concern to demonstrate my loyalty to feminist scholarship effectively precluded other loyalties. I assumed that an author must be *either* critical, amassing evidence to support her critical approach and ignoring evidence that disputed it, *or* sympathetic, neglecting to notice the context and "effective history" of texts and images that *have been used*, and *can be used*, to harm women.[10] *Can* the same historian be critical and sympathetic simultaneously? This was the challenge with which my scholarship engaged from this time on.

---

9. In the parlance of the 1980s, "Women's Studies" denoted the academic study of women and their circumstances, while "feminism" referred to a political stance.

10. Mary Daly's criterion for rejecting texts and images that harm women.

RECOLLECTIONS AND RECONSIDERATIONS

"The Body and Human Values in Augustine of Hippo,"
Augustinian Heritage 33:1 (1987) 57–70

> I came to understand ... through my own experience.[11]

After publishing my dissertation, *Augustine on the Body*, I received a kindly admonition from the Harvard Divinity School Dean, Krister Stendahl. Dean Stendahl told me that I had worked enough on "the body" and should now "move on" to more important topics. But I was not done with "the body." I still had not found the "intelligent body"—or better, "intelligent bodies." I needed a model that did not represent persons as components, body and mind/soul/spirit, thus inviting the quick hierarchical association of mind/soul with the male, and body with the female. I wanted to explore "the body" as inseparable—even indistinguishable—from mind/soul. But I had no word with which to designate *one* irreducible entity, not analyzable into components.

In retrospect, Augustine noticed his unrelenting quest for happiness and the *unhappiness* that he experienced as a direct result of that quest. He recalled *only* his unhappiness, identifying unhappiness as a *physical* condition like insomnia or an itching scab.[12] Centuries later, Freud also valued unhappiness. Both authors recognized that if a person is happy *enough*, he is unlikely to *change*. Nothing but persistent unhappiness of a certain intensity generates the energy for change.

In this essay I used the term "sexual preference," implying, as later was emphatically pointed out to me, that a person *chooses* or "prefers" certain sexual objects and acts. I now understand that this term does not adequately represent the experience of people who insist that they were born with a sexual "orientation" other than heteronormativity. I also tried to discuss too much in the essay, from Augustine's "conversion"—why is it in quotation marks in the essay?—to his most difficult doctrine, original sin.

The complexity and beauty of Augustine's ideas and their rootedness in his particular experience are well-described in the essay, but I also criticized his assumption that his experience was universal and could be predicated of every human being. I fault the *effective history*[13] of his failure to urge Christians to "work toward just social arrangements *now*, sexual

---

11. Augustine, *Confessions*, 8.5.
12. Augustine too needed "intelligent bodies!"
13. Hans-Georg Gadamer's phrase for the history of the *uses* of an idea.

equality *now*, and affirmation of the beauty and goodness of sexuality," and his despair of the world we inhabit *now* in favor of an imagined world beyond the present life.

"Hermeneutics of Generosity and Suspicion: Pluralism and Theological Education," 1987

In this article I endeavored to imagine the changes needed in theological education to address the "new pluralism"—meaning new people, people whose perspectives have not been part of theological education—who are presently asking new questions. I described experiments in the Theology Doctoral Colloquium and Common Doctoral seminar at Harvard Divinity School, in which students and faculty together sought alternatives to the traditional goal of "rational transcendence of differences." The *style of the discourse* was critical. Rejecting the scholarly method in which each participant forwards his own argument by attacking others' perspectives, assumptions, and arguments, we sought to work collaboratively rather than competitively.

The article contains many questions the Theology faculty found useful for opening discussion to a wide range of perspectives, to people with vastly different life experiences, people who had not had access in Western institutions to "reality defining" discourse. It was a start, but Christianity was assumed to be the common denominator. I had not yet begun to think about how to generate fruitful discussion with "people of other religions," focusing instead on the social issues confronting our dominantly Christian institution, society, and culture.[14]

"Revisioning an Embodied Christianity," *Unitarian Universalist Christian* 42 (1987)

The *practice* and sensory engagement of Christian worship demonstrates the centrality of bodies in the religion of the "Word made flesh." But because human bodies have been considered peripheral, the Incarnation of Jesus Christ has not been given theological centrality. Because Christians

---

14. Professor Diana Eck, one of the founders of dialogue with "other" religions at Harvard, declined to use the phrase, "other religions," because of its assumption that Christianity holds the central place in any discussion. "We are all 'other' to each other," she said in a 2016 conversation at Grace Cathedral, San Francisco.

have considered assent to creeds and doctrines central, theology is distorted. The identification of "person" as hierarchically *stacked components* underlies dismissal of body as integral.[15] Lacking the concept of an "intelligent body," the Incarnation did not carry its full weight for Christians. The Incarnation meant that the intelligent body is no longer merely flesh, but spirit, life, and truth.

The essay attempted to identify both resources for the present and the assumptions and commitments that hinder recognition of the significance of body. I tried to adjust the balance between the considerable attention to cultivating "soul" and theologians' slender attention to the significance of body and the rich meaning of the Incarnation.

"Pilgrimage as Metaphor in a Nuclear Age," *Theology Today*, 1988

The metaphor of Christian life as a pilgrimage demonstrates the ambiguous Christian understanding of "the world." On the one hand, "God *so loved* the world"; on the other hand, Christian texts frequently describe "the world" as a strange, alien, and dangerous place. The American spiritual says it succinctly: "This world is not my home, I'm just a-passin' through."

My publications of 1987–88 occurred in the context of a "nuclear world," a world threatened with destruction. Awareness of this fact of life gave urgency to life and thought, a sense that we do not banquet at ease with the Olympian gods, but make our slippery lives under newly dangerous conditions. Threats to human life are perennial, but we sensed the fragility and vulnerability of human life in a new way. The "nuclear age," became a symbol for the dangers and pain of the contemporary world.

Presently, nuclear weapons do not occupy a large role in public fears; American media—and thus the popular imagination—consider terrorism to be more immediately threatening. But nuclear danger has not disappeared. In July 2016, newspapers reported that North Korea considers United States' embargoes because of human rights violations a "declaration of war." North Korea continues to stockpile and test nuclear weapons in 2017.

Devotional manuals regard sufferings of all kinds as "trials." Christians are admonished to trust that God, who knows what we are able to

---

15. Thomas Aquinas taught that different entities cannot occupy the same metaphysical niche; see my discussion in *The Word Made Flesh*, 168–69, 172–73.

bear, will send only the afflictions that ultimately strengthen a Christian. This belief may help individuals to bear suffering, but it is egregiously untheological. Most Christians do not believe that God designs and delivers pain to punish, test, or "strengthen" Christians. The African American novelist Toni Morrison comments:

> When Violet's mother, Rose Dear, and her five children are abandoned and evicted, neighbors bring what they can spare, along with advice: "Don't let this whip you, Rose. You got us, Rose Dear. . . . He ain't given you nothing you can't bear, Rose." But had He? Maybe this one time He had. Had misjudged and misunderstood her particular backbone. This one time. This here particular spine.[16]

Gendered instruction for living a Christian life is nowhere more evident than in devotional manuals. *The Pilgrim's Progress*, a best-seller for several centuries, is not subtle on this point. When the Interpreter instructs the protagonist, Christian, on how he must live the Christian life, he is outfitted with armor, given weapons, and taught to fight. Later, when his wife, Christiana, sets out on her pilgrimage, the Interpreter takes her to a slaughter-house where a sheep is being slaughtered. He tells Christiana, "You must learn of this sheep to suffer, and to put up with wrongs without murmurings or complaints. Behold how quietly she takes her death, and without objecting, she suffereth her skin to be pulled over her ears."[17]

A developed and exercised religious life should, I believe, question and offer alternatives to the socialization of men and women in secular society. Instructions on the practice of a life "before God" should not reinforce or strengthen socialized attitudes and behavior.

In the fifteenth century criticisms of literal pilgrimages became numerous. Devotional manuals like *The Pilgrim's Progress* began to describe an *interior* pilgrimage to the "Celestial City." The article explores whether—and how—pilgrimage could be a useful metaphor for Christian life. A lifetime of learning all that one needs to know to be a useful and happy human being can be symbolized as a pilgrimage across time. And many modern pilgrims still traverse the Great Pilgrimage to Santiago and other ancient pilgrimage routes. They testify that pilgrimage across space can still be a useful practice for gaining spiritual focus and growth.

16. Morrison, *Jazz*, 99.
17. Bunyan, *Pilgrim's Progress*, 210.

RECOLLECTIONS AND RECONSIDERATIONS

Practicing Christianity: Critical Perspectives for an Embodied Spirituality, 1988

This book, and the course that preceded it, responded to an allegation that Harvard Divinity School failed to form students' spirituality. This was not an inaccurate observation, but this "failure" was, in fact, a carefully thought-through strategy. Since the student body was comprised of women and men of a range of Christian denominations, with a significant number of students of other world religions and no religion, faculty thought it presumptuous to attempt to shape students' particular spiritualities. Rather, our commitment was to providing the tools and methods that would enable students to shape their own religious lives.

The course explored the popular best-sellers, self-help manuals of the Christian West. Devotional manuals were written for Christians who were neither learned nor theologically trained. The course had three agenda: "To explore historical interpretations of Christian life; to analyze the values that inform these interpretations; and to develop a critical method for constructing a contemporary religious practice." In lectures I approached devotional manuals both sympathetically and critically.

Students who enrolled in the class had different interests. Some were interested in using devotional manuals for their own religious practice; these students were impatient and annoyed with the critical questions I brought to the texts. They needed to be convinced that discernment was important. I invoked Martin Luther who, when confronted with a scriptural "proof-text," replied, "I know that is the Word of God, but is it the Word of God *to me*?" Other students came to the course seeking confirmation of their prior rejection of the manuals' values and instructions.

Discussion sections were contentious. I hoped to persuade students of both perspectives to entertain the others' perspectives. Sometimes this worked, sometimes not. I never taught the course again; instead, I wrote the book.

How should Christians live? Devotional manuals proposed answers to this question that were based on assumptions, values, and preferred styles of personal and social relationships. Yet these background topics were not discussed in the manuals themselves. Rather, they were embedded in advocacy of certain attitudes and practices. Most instructions address readers who, for example, are able to give to the poor, who can *choose* to fast, and who have comforts from which they can abstain for limited times. Income inequality is presumed; involuntary poverty is assumed; voluntary poverty is praised.[18]

An enemy against which to struggle was considered indispensable for constructing and maintaining a religious life. Naming the enemy is high on their agenda. One cannot study Christian devotional manuals without noticing that a great deal of energy is to be amassed by positing a hostile friction between "something called body and something called soul."[19] This discord, so intimate, constant, and strong, was thought to generate a great deal of tensile energy. A model of "person" as stacked components of unequal value underlay devotional manuals' instructions. A parallel enmity is posited between the individual and society. In devotional manuals, societies are seldom thought of as needing—and worthy of— Christians' critical attention, care, and revision. The closer the identified evil, whether one's own recalcitrant body or sinful society, the more alert and prepared the Christian must be. Authors of devotional manuals believed that evil exists and must be fought.

Can Christians do without an enemy? The designation of an enemy or enemies is based on fear. Augustine suggested an alternative. He identified evil not as an active independent force—an enemy—but as *deprivation of good*. There is, in Augustine's understanding, literally "no such *thing* as evil."[20] Evil is *nothing but* corruption of good. Deprived of *all* good, created beings "will cease to exist altogether."[21] What we are admonished to do, according to Augustine, is to "carry over" the weight or energy of the soul from fear to love. Evil can be overcome, not by fighting it, but by building good, motivated by love. For Augustine, *this activity defines the Christian life*.

In *Practicing Christianity* I did not differentiate between the advice of authors of devotional manuals and theologians. Theologians often gave practical instructions in Christian living, but authors of devotional manuals simplified instructions, intending their writings to be used by people not equipped to understand theologians' often more complex instructions. For example: Augustine (in the West), and Gregory Palamas (in the East), teach that the soul's "passionate forces" must not be "put to death," but

---

18. Christians seem not to have worried about involuntary poverty until John Wesley raised funds for helping poor people improve their circumstances by starting a business.

19. Sheets-Johnstone, *Corporeal Turn*, 20.

20. Augustine, *Confessions*, 7.13.

21. Augustine, *Confessions*, 7.12.

rather must be "carried over" (Augustine's term, *fero*[22]), "transformed and sanctified" (Gregory's term[23]) to love for "the neighbor in God." Nothing is to be destroyed or lost in this transfer of energy.

Devotional manuals demonstrate no such subtlety. "Kill" is the word used most often when they describe how to manage "fleshly hankerings." A sixteenth-century Lutheran children's catechism offers the following pedagogical advice: "Use the knife of God's Word to cut off the branches of their contumacious will. Raise them in the fear of God. And when their wild nature comes up again—as weeds always will—and the old Adam sins in them again, kill it and bury it deep in the ground . . ."[24] Devotional manuals tend to omit both sophisticated arguments and doctrinal warrants, appealing instead to popularly accessible images. Such simplifications create distortions that affect attitudes and values.

"Imitation of Christ: Is it Possible in the Twentieth Century?" *The Princeton Theological Bulletin*, 1989

Devotional manuals frequently advise that Christian life is best understood as imitation of Christ. But imitation of Christ can be practiced in several different ways. It can be practiced as meditation on the inner life and passion of Christ (Thomas à Kempis); as participation in Christ's divinity, or deification (Gregory of Nyssa); as adopting the poverty, humility, powerlessness, and vulnerability of the historical Jesus (St. Francis of Assisi); or as imitation of the feelings of the scriptural characters who surrounded Jesus (*Meditations on the Life of Christ*). I argued that none of these interpretations of how a Christian should practice imitation of Christ can be adopted without reinterpretation.

I struggled for many years to find value in the devotional manuals of the Christian traditions. I have avoided the question of whether the harm done by their suggestions exceeds the pockets of insight and usefulness for the living of a Christian life. I now see, however, that devotional manuals have advocated or encouraged a great deal of suffering. There is wheat among the chaff, but sorting one from the other requires two activities that most people are unable or unwilling to do. First: one must reconstruct the historical moment (in all its complexity—social assumptions, gender

---

22. Augustine, *Confessions*, 13.9.
23. Palamas, *Homily*, 209.
24. Quoted by Strauss in Trinkhaus and Obermann, *The Pursuit of Holiness*, 291.

arrangements and many other factors) *in the context of which* (some? most?) people (seem to have) valued devotional instructions. One must ask the "whom did it serve?" and "on whose backs was it built?" questions. Second, the difficult work of individual and communal discernment is required.

Historians can seldom know enough about the original audience to judge whether a belief or practice was helpful in the historical moment and circumstance of its proposal. We must accept that devotional manuals would not have been preserved if they were not found useful. We can, however, with diligence and discernment, examine our own circumstances, both personal and social, to determine whether the belief or practice is "the word of God *to me*," *to us*, in our circumstances. If, for example, the metaphor of Christian life as imitation of Christ seems promising, inspiring, or useful, can it be interpreted in a way that maximizes its fruitfulness for *my* life in *my* circumstances, avoiding its potential dangers? Michel Foucault said: "Everything is dangerous, which is not exactly the same thing as bad. If everything is dangerous, then we always have something to do."[25] Certainly, if we seek to appropriate admonitions of devotional manuals, "we always have something to do."

One value strongly advocated by historical devotional manuals that *is* useful for contemporary Americans is that of activity. In twenty-first-century North American media culture, passivity and entertainment are encouraged. Devotional manuals contest the assumption that we should simply react as best we can to "whatever happens." We can, without scrupulosity and with responsibility and gratitude, accept the challenge of *making* a life informed by chosen values. "The metaphor of imitation of Christ can provide, not a blueprint that can be automatically applied, but a challenge and an inspiration to twentieth-century Christians to engage our clearest self-knowledge and our most perceptive analysis of the situation in which we must act in beginning to ask ourselves, How might I imitate Christ in *this* moment?"

Carnal Knowing: Female Nakedness and Religious Meaning in the Christian West, 1989

Naked human bodies carried many meanings in the Christian West. Nakedness symbolized innocence or shame, vulnerability or culpability, worthlessness or great value, beauty or ugliness. Yet, it is evident that negative

---

25. Foucault, quoted in Dreyful and Rabinow, *Michel Foucault*, 231–32.

meanings of nakedness are overwhelmingly associated with the female body, while strength, virility, discipline, and heroic action are associated with male bodies. From the figure of Eve forward, women represented lust, sin, and death.[26] Part I of *Carnal Knowing* discusses the social and religious practices in which women were naked in public places. Part II discusses images and literary descriptions of female nakedness. In sum, public representations "dissociated women's bodies from women as subjects of their experience and represented them as figures in a male drama."[27] Women who actively developed religious commitment were said to "become male." "For women, courage, conscious choice, and self-possession constituted gender transgression."

By the term "carnal knowing" I intended to indicate "an activity in which the intimate interdependence and irreducible convergence of thinking, feeling, sensing, and understanding is revealed." The third-century North African Christian Tertullian vividly describes this activity.

> The soul alone is so far from conducting the affairs of life that we do not withdraw from community with the flesh even our thoughts, ... since whatever is done in the heart is done by the soul in the flesh and through the flesh.... But if you allow that the faculty which rules the senses and which they call the *hegemonikon* has its sanctuary in the brain, or wheresoever the philosophers are pleased to locate it, *the flesh will still be the thinking place of the soul.*[28]

Rereading this book, I am pleasantly surprised by the scope and variety of knowledges I engaged. I used to know a lot! Presently, I have forgotten a lot! Theory and details are clear and well chosen. I should, however, have highlighted the only generic use of "woman" I have found in patristic literature rather than burying it in a footnote! In CE 431, the all-male Council of Ephesus established the designation of Mary as Theotokos. Emphasizing her humanity as well as her status as "God-bearing," they stated, "The Blessed Virgin was woman as we are."[29]

---

26. It was incorrect to say that "original sin was not associated with sex until the 16th century." This association was already clear in Augustine in the early fifth century.

27. A sentence on page 3 of the Introduction should read: "The prostitute raises Enkidu above the beasts, and Siduri reduces Gilgamesh from a god. These women define the lower and upper limits of the human."

28. Tertullian, *De anima*, 11.1; my emphasis.

29. Schaff, *Nicene and Post-Nicene Fathers*, vol. 14, 225.

If women's perspectives are to influence society, two conditions that have not existed in Western history must be present. There must be *collective voice in the public sphere*. Small gatherings of women in private spaces cannot achieve influence in society and its institutions. In 1989 when *Carnal Knowing* was published it was difficult to imagine that the necessary conditions might exist in my lifetime. Many circumstances still undermine hope. But the first woman presidential candidate to be nominated by a major political party ran for office in 2016. Her opponent successfully disqualified and effectively humiliated her and all who share her gender. Nevertheless, her nomination brought women a step closer to collective voice in the public sphere.

"Infancy, Parenting, and Nourishment in Augustine's *Confessions*," *The Hunger of the Heart: Reflections on the Confessions of Augustine*, 1991

> When I listen to a patient I am not reconstructing the "facts" of a case history but listening for patterns, strains of feeling, and associations that may move us out of painful repetitions and into articulated understanding.[30]

This essay considers the *Confessions*, Augustine's "journal," as therapy. Augustine addresses God, the ultimate "therapist," but he is also aware that readers will be interested in his self-revelation. Nevertheless, the tone of anxious introspection is a clue that his primary engagement is with himself; he is *by himself*. Writing his confessions, Augustine practiced Socratic dialectic, a "soundless dialogue between me and myself."[31] Augustine's self-therapy, however, is not simply the case history we expect from contemporary therapy. In the last three books of the *Confessions* he also located the self in history and cosmos, time and space.

Augustine anticipated Freud's interest in earliest infancy, in the responses that will become habitual, directing the infant's developing personality. God's first act in Augustine's life was provision of the nursing breast: "neither my mother nor my nurses filled their own breasts with milk; it was you [God] who, through them, gave me the food of my infancy."[32]

---

30. Hustvedt, *The Sorrows of an American*, 80.
31. Arendt, *Thinking*, 185.
32. Augustine, *Confessions*, 1.6.

Augustine received his mother's milk: "All I knew was how to suck, to be content with bodily pleasure and to be discontented with bodily pain; that was all."[33]

The besetting problem of self-analysis is evident in the *Confessions*, namely, simultaneous privileged access and limitation of perspective. Augustine saw *concupiscentia* at its most undisguised in the infant's behavior. The infant *acts as if he fears* that if he did not demand caregivers' attention, he would not receive necessary care and nourishment. Freud's insight that life can go forward *only* from the "place" at which it was arrested requires the patient to re-member and relive the occasion of traumatic stress—presumably the trauma of birth—altering the original response. Translating Freud into religious language, we could say that: the patient must be "born again," facing again the traumatic shock and moving *through* it. Augustine experienced his conversion as a "rebirth." He replaced his parents—the anxious mother, Monnica, with Mother Church, and the ineffective father, Patricius, with Father God. No longer "licking at shadows," Augustine is nourished and satisfied: "What am I at my best, except an infant suckling the milk you give and feeding on you, the food that is incorruptible?"[34]

"'If I Perish, We Perish': A Collective Interpretation of Competition," 1991

I encouraged students to collaborate on writing projects, a procedure common to scientists but rare in the humanities. Unaccustomed to collaboration, students found the process difficult; from choosing collaborators to distributing portions of research and writing, every step of the way carried potential problems. Does collaboration produce stronger results, as scientists seem to think? Under the best circumstances, yes. But for the inexperienced, the problem of shirkers, personality conflicts, and disagreements sometimes outweighed the advantages. I had never collaborated on a writing project, so in order to experience both the advantages and problems, I proposed a collaborative project in which I participated.

Seven women doctoral students and I examined and reflected on our experiences of competition in the academy. We met frequently in the summer of 1990 to talk about our often painful experiences. Sometimes we cried. Harvard University seemed to us to be dedicated to competitive

---

33. Augustine, *Confessions*, 1.6.
34. Augustine, *Confessions*, 4.1.

learning, its pedagogy based on the conviction that fierce competition produced "cutting edge" learning.

We found, somewhat to our surprise, that we did not want to advocate *replacing* competition with cooperation. Respectful competition is zestful, allowing ideas to be refined, rendering them nuanced and precise. We recognized the importance of "critical friends" who can identify weakness in an argument and suggest how it could be strengthened. Nevertheless, in classes and seminars in which the male model of competition is uncontested, women are often intimidated into silence. Even if we gather courage to speak we are often ignored; frequently discussion continues without any acknowledgement of our interventions.

Nevertheless, cooperation was not our ideal. We recognized that we would not be well served by receiving nothing but encouragement and praise. Instead, we suggested strategies to modify the atmosphere of competition. For example, we recognized that most men are more eager to be heard in the classroom than are most women. We agreed that when a woman speaks, another woman must reiterate and respond to her point so it is heard and included in the discussion, not summarily dropped.

We concluded that rather than advocating *either* competition or cooperation we wanted something more difficult to define, namely a *practice* of listening and speaking by which participants can achieve *together* understandings that cannot be achieved without *both* collaboration *and* competition. This practice includes critical suggestions that refine and strengthen rather than undermine. The goal is not that participants must come to agreement, but that each must be heard, acknowledged, considered, and responded to respectfully.

Classroom dynamics do not occur in an artificially enclosed "safe space" or "level playing field." Inevitably, they reflect and reiterate the attitudes and behavior of society outside the classroom. To ignore the "politics" of everyday life by claiming a space that excludes them does nothing but disallow analysis and reflection on classroom interactions. Classrooms are thick with politics. Students are aware that their futures depend to a significant extent on their classroom behavior. Each hopes to attract the approving notice of the teacher, who is very likely to be asked for a letter of recommendation in the future. In fact, the *only* person in the room who has the luxury of ignoring the politics of the classroom is the teacher, whose power in the situation is virtually unassailable. Teachers who claim that their classroom is "safe space" or a "level playing field" speak only for themselves; they mislead students. Fortunately, most students are too smart to believe this.

Augostino "Le Confessioni, 1991. Desire and Delight: A New Reading of Augustine's Confessions, 1992

>We catch fire and we go![35]

The Italian publisher, Landau, in Turin, Italy, asked me to write a commentary on Augustine's *Confessions* for a series the press was publishing. I accepted the invitation and wrote the small book—in English. My Italian was not up to the job, so the manuscript was translated and published first in Italian. The English version was published a year later.

Writing this book revealed to me that the circumstances of writing profoundly influence interpretation. I wrote copious notes by hand when I was on vacation on the Greek island of Paros with three friends. In the mornings I read the *Confessions* in Latin; afternoons we went to one of the many beautiful beaches surrounding Paros. Gazing at the azure Mediterranean, I pondered the morning's reading, excitedly making notes. In the evenings we ate, drank, and talked. The pleasure I was experiencing on this beautiful island alerted me both to the pleasure of reading Augustine's colorful Latin and Augustine's search for pleasure, the subject of his text. The *Confessions* "produce in the reader a responsive kaleidoscope of feeling—gratification, denial, frustration, discomfort, and satisfaction."[36] To my knowledge, no one had described Augustine's *Confessions* as a text of pleasure, a book about getting and keeping the greatest possible pleasure.[37]

The extraordinary power and beauty of Augustine's text clashes with its "exclusionary strategies," its authoritarianism, and its frequent failure to satisfy readers —withholding the name of his partner of more than a decade, for example. At moments in the text, he indulges in labored analysis, such as his description of his boyhood theft of pears. Most readers across the centuries have chosen to ignore *either* the beauty or the problems of the *Confessions*. But the beauty is *in* the complexity. Beauty and problems must somehow be seen simultaneously—not an easy task—as irreducible to the honest story of this complicated man.

35. Augustine, *Confessions*, 13.9.
36. Miles, *Desire and Delight*, 10.
37. Barthes, *Pleasure of the Text*.

My title, *Desire and Delight*, identifies the organizing theme of the *Confessions* as Augustine's *search for pleasure*. I found in the first nine books a vivid narrative, rich with particular people, their idiosyncrasies, and the colorful situations in which they lived and related to one another. That vividness, that particularity, seemed lacking in the later books in which Augustine ponders such topics as the nature of time, creation, and his duties as a bishop. His conversion, described in book eight, seemed to me simultaneously to end his search for pleasure and the pleasure of his text. His post-conversion life seemed not as engaging as his account of his youth, its temptations, interests, and urgencies.

Two decades later, my failure of vision was properly criticized by the several authors of *Seducing Augustine: Bodies, Desires, Confessions*.[38] Working with the rubric "desire" rather than "pleasure," they describe the latter books of the *Confessions* as the transformation of Augustine's fear-based *concupiscence* into vividly satisfying *concupiscentia* for God.

Writing the book I did not yet notice that Augustine described his conversion *not* as obliterating—stamping out, killing—the *force* of *concupiscentia*, but as "carrying over" *that very force* into desire for an ultimately satisfying object. Augustine advocated gathering the tremendous *energy*, the *urgency* of lust, and using that *power*—with God's help—to transform lust *into* love, into participation in God-is-Love. The *"weight"* of concupiscence was redistributed to the love project he described in *Confessions* 13.9.

Distracted by Augustine's dramatic conversion, narrated in *Confessions* book 8, many readers miss this essential point. His famous conversion ignores the long process by which he turned—God turned him, he says—from lust to love, *from* compulsive anxious grasping in the *fear* that something would be missed; *through* getting over himself a bit: "I relaxed a little from myself";[39] *to* "I breathe a little in you, God";[40] to his claim, "My weight is my love; by it I am carried wherever I am carried."[41] In short, as the authors of *Seducing Augustine* pointed out, the final books do not describe a diminishment of pleasure, but a new and more trustworthy kind of pleasure. Rather than the quasi-pleasure of satisfying a repetition compulsion—"licking at shadows" in Augustine's rich metaphor[42]—he experienced

---

38. Burrus, Jordan, and Mackendrick, *Seducing Augustine*.
39. "*cessavi de me paululum*." Augustine, *Confessions*, 7.14.
40. "*respire in te paululum*." Augustine, *Confessions*, 13.14.
41. Augustine, *Confessions*, 13.9.
42. Augustine, *Confessions*, 9.4.

a deeply trustworthy pleasure. He described this pleasure as *relaxing, rather than intensified struggle.*

In the final books of *Confessions*, Augustine examines several questions, *exploring*, not seeking final answers.[43] Content that his God knows the answers, he is less interested in the answers than in the questions. The questions have shifted subtly; they are no longer: What is memory? or what is time?, but *what do I think? What do I think* memory is? (book 10), *what do I think* time is? (book 11), and *how do I think* God did the work of creation? (book 12). *These* questions are not answerable; they are pleasurable explorations. Augustine *can know* what he thinks! (This is what writing is good for!) With relief he acknowledges that there is often no single right answer, either in scripture or in philosophy. This is serious play, not compulsive urgency as was his earlier anguished investigation of the origin of evil (book 7).

The affective quality of Augustine's post-conversion pleasure has changed from "hard slavery"[44] to "sweetness" (*suavitas, dulcedo*):

> How sweet (*suave*) it suddenly became to me to be without the sweetness (*suavatitibus*) of those empty toys! How glad I was to give up the things I had been so afraid to lose! For you cast them out from me, you true and supreme sweetness (*summa suavitas*); you cast them out and you entered into me to take their place, sweeter (*dulcior*) than all pleasure (*voluptate*), brighter than all light, but more inward than all hidden depths.[45]

"Theory, Theology, and Episcopal Church Women," *Women of the Protestant Mainline: A Case Study of the Episcopal Church in the Twentieth Century*, 1992

Catherine Prelinger, editor of *Women of the Protestant Mainline*, gathered twelve women—priests, historians, administrators, professors, and a librarian—to discuss and write essays on the subject of the ambiguous role of women in the notoriously patriarchal Episcopal Church in North America. The authors examined "religion and gender as part of a broader social fabric," questioning the traditional "universality" of men and the

---

43. A Socratic dialogue within himself.
44. Augustine, *Confessions*, 8.5.
45. Augustine, *Confessions*, 9.1.

"particularity" of women. In the Christian churches in general, and the Episcopal Church in particular, women have been placed in a position of "privileged subordination."

Ironically, activities and roles considered "natural" for women have been central to Christian practice: self-abnegation, self-sacrifice, humility, attentiveness to others' needs, obedience, and submissiveness. Yet these perceived "female characteristics" have not led to leadership roles for women in the churches that claim to value these characteristics highly.

Former studies of mainline Protestantism focused on church leadership, thus ensuring that, in male designed and administered institutions, women's participation was invisible. Women who participated in the Episcopal Church at the time of writing were lay women. Conducted over several years prior to the book's publication, the conversations were irreducibly *in media res*.[46] Since 1992, when *Women of the Protestant Mainline* was published, many women have been ordained and several have become bishops. Authors of essays in the volume disagreed about the potential significance of women's increasing participation at both clergy and laity levels. Several authors celebrate women's gradually increasing leadership roles; others are "skeptical about any real gender change in the church and point to the many pockets of institutional [gendered] oppression" remaining.

The intense conversations on which this volume was built did not seek—or achieve—consensus, a strength of the volume. Questions and issues surrounding women's participation and support of the Episcopal Church were raised, debated, and largely remain as questions and issues in the essays. Yet, clarifying issues and spelling out and examining differing perspectives represent important steps for the future of women in the Episcopal Church. Until quite recently women clergy have felt the need to prove themselves capable of managing the multiple leadership tasks of the church. It remains to be seen whether and how the increased participation of women clergy and laity will *change* the Episcopal Church.

---

46. A significant mark of the book's location in the middle of an ongoing conversation is the reference to Church of England women as not yet permitted ordination to the priesthood. The first woman was ordained in 1994.

Recollections and Reconsiderations

"The Revelatory Body: Signorelli's 'Resurrection of the Flesh' at Orvieto," *Theological Education*, 1992

Originally a lecture at a conference on art and religion at the Graduate Theological Union, this essay honors Professor Jane Daggett Dillenberger for her pioneering work in religion and art history. The subject of the lecture had personal as well as professional interest for Professor Dillenberger. Like Signorelli, she had lost a young son some years ago.

I examined the social, religious, and artistic convergence that informed Signorelli's vivid representation of the resurrection of bodies. Presumably, the subject was chosen by church authorities who commissioned the painting of the San Brizio Chapel of the Orvieto Cathedral, Orvieto, Italy. Because neither experience nor example of resurrected bodies can inform paintings, the subject engaged the painter's imagination as perhaps no other subject. St. Augustine's explicitly imaginary description of the bodily resurrection in *City of God* XXII seems to have informed Signorelli's vision. Augustine described resurrected bodies as weightless and without sexual urgency, "enjoying each other's beauty for itself alone." Signorelli supplied the visual details; unselfconsciously naked bodies climb from graves in different stages of enfleshment.

Art historical analyses that omit religious motivation cannot do justice to church paintings, commissioned by clergy. The Orvieto Signorelli paintings picture—and enable viewers to imagine—events occurring at the end of the world, and to imagine themselves participating in these vivid scenes. The figures of Fra Angelico and Signorelli stand at the left of the Antichrist scene on the right wall of the San Brizio Chapel; they were contemporaries (at the time of painting) whose presence invites viewers into the scene.

At the beginning of the sixteenth century, when Signorelli was painting at Orvieto, the "period eye"[47] saw the beauty of human bodies as the apex of created beauty. Half a century later, naked bodies would be symbolic of sex, sin, and death. Both perspectives are scriptural; throughout the history of Christianity, bodies have migrated between interpretations. The Genesis 1 account of creation places humans as the summit and crown of creation. But in Genesis 3, Adam and Eve's nakedness symbolizes sinful humanity. Complex factors were involved in the dramatic change in the interpretation of bodies after Signorelli painted his "Resurrection," but a watershed was established by the December 1563 meeting of the Council of Trent in which

---

47. Baxandall's phrase in *Painting and Experience*.

the Council banned "unsuitable subjects" (*incommodus*) from church art, an order that was immediately understood to refer to naked bodies.

Why does one culture "see" bodies as God's beautiful creation, and another "see" naked bodies as inherently sinful? I suggest that visual associations within the culture are decisive. If naked bodies are familiar, a part of daily life—living and dying bodies, women's bodies giving birth and feeding children at the breast, sick and wounded; bodies, in the home, in the marketplace, in churches—bodies are likely to be seen as beautiful. If a society sees naked bodies in public only as pornography at the corner newsstand, bodies are likely to be associated with sex and sin. The so-called "Father of pornography," Pietro Aretino, was the first to complain about the naked bodies in Michelangelo's "Last Judgment" in the Sistine Chapel, leading to their repeated overpainting in the sixteenth, seventeenth, and eighteenth centuries.

At the beginning of the sixteenth century, however, Signorelli insisted that unclothed human bodies, male and female, "both are, and can be represented as, the site and symbol of religious subjectivity, aspiration, and achievement."

"Santa Maria Maggiore's Fifth-Century Mosaics: Triumphal Christianity and the Jews," *Harvard Theological Review*, 1993

I was on sabbatical leave from Harvard Divinity School in 1983 to 1984. I lived in Rome less than a block from Santa Maria Maggiore and I visited the church's fifth-century mosaics daily. Because of their height on the clerestory level and the dust that coated them, I strained to see them. Imagine, then, my delight on Christmas morning when I entered the church to find them lighted—still dusty, but much more visible. I saw them again in 1990 when they had been cleaned. To the spectator passing in front of them, their tiny tesserae set to catch the light made the figures appear to move. They were utterly beautiful.

In the mid-fifth century when the mosaics were set in place, they were part of a movement operating from myriad points within Roman society to exclude and ostracize Jews from public life. This message was in the mosaics' placement in Santa Maria Maggiore. Moving up the nave toward the altar, the mosaics depicted stories from the Hebrew Bible describing God's covenant and care for the Jewish people. They culminate in the apse mosaics that present scenes of the birth and infancy of Jesus. The mosaics, and the supersessionist story they told, were in Santa Maria Maggiore, a central place of Christian power. As described in my article, the story they told was reiterated by sermons, laws, and popular violence against Jewish synagogues.

Social power is gathered and consolidated by the designation of an enemy. By the mid-fifth century, Christianity, which originated as a sect within Judaism, repositioned Judaism as other, as enemy. The closer the designated enemy, the stronger the power gained by struggle against it. Judaism, the sibling of Christianity, remained an ideal enemy for many centuries in the dominantly Christian West.

Michel Foucault identified two kinds of power; he called the power to coerce "weak power." Weak power is used only when "strong power," the power to attract, fails. In this essay I discussed new exclusionary laws and the destruction of temples by mobs as "weak power" exerted to marginalize Jews. The Santa Maria Maggiore fifth-century mosaics represent "strong power," the power to attract to popular attitudes of hostility. Beauty is not innocent. Within its society of origin, spectators, admiring the beauty, absorb the political messages that slide across unnoticed.[48]

I gave a version of this article as a slide lecture at a conference on religion and art at the University of Hawaii. It was evident in the question period that the lecture had prompted a good deal of hostility. The objections, however, were not clear to me. I am still not sure whether hearers were disturbed by the systematic marginalization and oppression of Jews in fifth-century Rome, whether some objected to my demonstration that beautiful artworks were part of how supersessionism *worked*, or whether they were irate at my suggestion that Christians intentionally sought to establish a "new" religion by denigrating the ancient and honorable religion of Judaism. Or all of the above.

Moreover, several art historians objected to my placement of art works in the midst of public communications within historical communities, rather than leaving them on the pedestal on which they were thought to "belong." The traditional method of art history has been to analyze an artwork's formal qualities in relation to its place in a history of style. But presently many art historians are interested in the role artworks played in social, political, and religious debates; they seek to reconstruct artworks *in the life*, to identify their place in thick social conversations. Historical

---

48. Barthes, *The Pleasure of the Text*.

approaches bring an artwork off the wall, off the pedestal, and into the vivid life of a community, where (*I* think) it "belongs"!

"A Sea of Love: Marguerite Porete's 'A Mirror for Simple Souls,'" *The Christian* Century, 1993

Marguerite Porete had a strong vision of the world and human life for which she was willing to sacrifice her life. Prior to its publication she had sent her book, *A Mirror for Simple Souls,* to two clerical readers and a lay theologian, none of whom found fault with it. Yet it was subsequently condemned as containing fifteen erroneous beliefs. Confident of its legitimacy, Porete refused to recant or even to explain it further. She was burned as a heretic on June 1, 1310, at the Place de Grève in Paris. Ironically, in the centuries following her death her book circulated anonymously in five medieval translations and became a spiritual classic. Its author was not identified until 1946.

"Textual Harrassment: Desire and the Female Body," *The Good Body: Asceticism in Contemporary Culture*, 1994

This essay originated in a conference (and subsequent book) about contemporary eating disorders. I argued that eating disorders will prove intractable as long as "desire" is gendered male and women are understood as *objects* of male desire. Women's desire, I said, is slenderly understood and supported in American society. Eating disorders may be one response to a lack of "authorization" for women's desire. When eating disorders are understood as "the pleasure of no pleasure," a way of getting pleasure by default, more satisfying pleasures can be sought. These might involve "exercising and strengthening female desire, providing it with the support of multiple and diverse models, symbolic authorization, and a repertoire of textual warrants."

Recollections and Reconsiderations

"'*Jesus patabilis*': Augustine's Debate with the Manichaeans," *Faithful Imagining: Essays in Honor of Richard R. Niebuhr*, 1995

Can the sensitivities of the present provide a critical perspective for the illumination of historical texts and events? Can insight into contemporary issues be achieved from study of the past? Historians are uneasy with these questions, but this essay seeks to demonstrate that both questions can (cautiously) be answered positively.

At the end of the fourth century, Augustine of Hippo argued, against North African Manichaean Christians, that human responsibility is limited to the community of rational minds, by which he meant human beings. Manichaeans, on the other hand, taught that humans are part of a community of all living beings, and it is this larger community for which humans are responsible. Due to his rhetorical skill and institutional power, Augustine's view has dominated Western societies to our own time. "It is likely that if the Manichaean doctrine of a suffering Jesus 'hanging on every tree,' symbol of the struggle and suffering of the whole creation, had woven itself into mainstream Christianity, the exploitive anthropocentrism of Western societies might have been significantly modified."

The history of Christianity contains ideas and images that are needed in the twenty-first century. Often, however, as in the case of the Manichaeans, the needed resources come from branches of Christianity that have been labeled "heretical." Triumphant Christianity is not the whole of the Christian story. The history of Christianity to which we usually have access is a history of attempts to eliminate diversity in the interest of a unity that has never existed.[49] Indeed, that is *why* appeals for unity are ubiquitous. "Unity" *could* be redefined as including and enjoying diversity, but it is probably illusory to expect that the concept of unity as inclusive rather than exclusive can be rescued from its coercive history. Mary Daly's principle corrects the unrealistically optimistic effort to salvage every Christian idea and image: if a concept *has been* coercive and *can be* used coercively, it must be jettisoned rather than recovered.

---

49. See chapter 7 for further discussion of the problem of "unity" in the history of Christianity.

"Fashioning the Self," *The Christian Century*, 1995

The article is a review of Robert Altman's docudrama, "Ready-to-Wear." The movie, filmed at the *Prêt-a-Porter* Spring 1994 Collection in Paris, featured cameo appearances by many famous actors. Altman's apparent intention was to expose the implicit claim of the fashion industry to fashion the "self." Within his agenda, his "real questions" emphasized the superficiality of the fashion world. As in *The Pilgrim's Progress*, a seventeenth-century best-selling devotional manual, characters in the film are reduced to their vices.

As depicted by Altman, no one in the fashion industry has talent, works hard, or suffers. Most remarkably, at the height of the AIDS crises that was decimating the fashion industry, no one is ill, and safe sex is unheard of. Altman does not preach directly, but the film is a sermon. His caricature of the fashion world makes his point—not subtly—that fashion is incapable of providing the resources for shaping the desires and identities of individuals and communities. The film makes Altman's point, but it is argued tendentiously.

"Happiness in Motion: Desire and Delight," *In Pursuit of Happiness: Boston University Studies in Philosophy and Religion*, 1995

Historical descriptions of happiness have largely overlooked, diminished, and disrespected bodies. In fact, the obvious vulnerability of human bodies has prompted the search for a kind of happiness that does not share this vulnerability. Ancient Greek philosophers thought that they found in rationality a happiness that is not at the mercy of "whatever happens." However, two "goods" are spectacularly missing from most historical accounts of happiness, namely, healthy bodies and just societies. Indeed, bodies' susceptibility to disease and accident, and the inevitability of unjust societies, are precisely why historical authors found it necessary to seek happiness that is not dependent on them. Responding to the question, What is the good life? Aristotle concluded, "The life according to reason is best and pleasantest, since reason more than anything else is human. This life is also the happiest."[50] He recommended contemplation as the activity by which happiness could be gained and maintained.

50. Aristotle, *Nichomachean Ethics*, 10.7.

Augustine's requirement for happiness was permanence, so he did not envision happiness as attainable in this life. Augustine distrusted the only sort of happiness granted to human beings, namely, happiness *now*, transient but vivid, "the silken weavings of our afternoons."[51] Deeply mistrustful of happiness *now*, he taught that eternal happiness was all that mattered. Similarly, for my fundamentalist father, only adversity was trustworthy; its purpose was to test faith, and it must be addressed with "girded loins." Happiness *now* merely increased a person's vulnerability to inevitable adversity. For my brother, suffering from depression, happiness was "stupid," ignoring as it must the reality of pain.

I suggest that happiness is produced by attentiveness to beauty *now*. To be happy, however, I must relinquish both permanence and perfection. These sacrifices may be thought of as "lowering expectations"—advice sometimes proposed by contemporary authors. But from another perspective, happiness *now* is accompanied by heightened expectations, namely, the expectation that beauty is both ubiquitous and remarkable. The release of unattainable conditions (permanence and perfection) permits us to notice what *belongs* to the one who can see it. Iris Murdoch wrote:

> Should we not . . . endeavor to see and attend to what surrounds and concerns us, because it is there and is interesting, beautiful, strange, worth experiencing, and because it demands (and *needs*) our attention, rather than living in a vague haze of private anxiety and fantasy?[52]

"Religion and Food: The Case of Eating Disorders," 1995

Food is integral to religious practice. But *not* eating in also significant. Understanding "person" as stacked components supported the rationale for fasting as "starving the body to feed the soul." "Person" was conceptualized as a closed energy system in which one component is strengthened and exercised at the direct expense of the other. Although Plato wrote, "Never exercise the body without the soul or the soul without the body," he pictured them (in this passage) as requiring balance and working closely together like the fingers and "opposable" thumb.[53]

---

51. Stephens, "Sunday Morning."
52. Murdoch, *Metaphysics*, 218.
53. Plato, *Timaeus*, 88c: "The mathematician or anyone else whose thoughts are much

Rather than the common assumptions that young women want to look like the thin models they see in media, or that they want to control *something*, I proposed that eating disorders need to be understood as proceeding from "thwarted desire." Eating disorders are a *social*, not an individual, problem, namely, the paucity of resources available to young women for designing—choosing and exercising—a rich subjectivity. Saul Bellow's protagonist in *Henderson the Rain King* has an inner voice that repeats "I want, I want," but will not say *what* it wants. In the seventeenth century, Thomas Traherne wrote, "We love we know not what, so everything allures us."[54]

Young women are not encouraged by North American public culture to "desperately seek" to shape their lives. "My body is too big" is a common refrain of girls and women with eating disorders—too big in the *culture*, too frequently displayed, positioned to attract male desire, too fetishized—disproportionate with women's unsupported subjectivity.

"Introduction," in *Sex, Priests, and Power: Anatomy of a Crisis*, by Richard Sipe, 1995

When I seek to understand an idea or a practice I first examine the original context in which it appeared. Often I can see why an idea or practice that seems to me presently unusable has been useful within its society of origin—at least for some members of that society. Having understood its attraction in other circumstances, I can then proceed to discern why it has become counter-productive or dangerous. In this article I seek to reconstruct why clerical celibacy seemed a good idea in its culture of origin, and why it has become harmful to contemporary priests and their sexual partners, whether consensual or coerced.[55]

Unfortunately, my pessimism about a book's effectiveness in creating social change is reinforced by *Sex, Priests, and Power*. Since its publication in 1995, the Roman Catholic Church has not relaxed its requirement of clergy celibacy. Despite Richard Sipe's careful analysis of the harms involved

---

absorbed in some intellectual pursuit, must allow his body also to have due exercise... and he who is careful to fashion the body should in turn impart to the soul its proper motions and should cultivate the arts and all philosophy."

54. Traherne, *Centuries*, IV. 16.

55. Sexual "partners" of priests are victims in the sense that due to priests' institutional loyalties, they are unable to provide the care, attention, and support needed by partners who are rendered emotionally, physically, and often financially vulnerable by their relationship.

in clergy celibacy, more than a decade after publication, the requirement is unchanged. Neither the massive human pain nor the enormous cost to churches of concealing and/or remunerating victims of clergy abuse has prompted rethinking and revision of clergy celibacy. Sipe adopts Martin Luther's perspective on celibacy, namely: celibacy is a gift, and a gift is to be admired—Sipe calls it "awesome"—a gift cannot, however, be legislated.[56]

"Seeing (as if) with Our Own Eyes: Vision and Spectatorship in Religion and Contemporary Film," *The Papers of the Henry Luce III Fellows in Theology*, 1996

The Henry Luce III Fellows in Theology volume began with a conference at Princeton University in which the selected "fellows" gave preliminary lectures on our proposed topics, became acquainted with one another, and benefitted from the suggestions of "critical friends." It was a rich collegial experience. Since we were in different fields of religious studies, we didn't experience the academic urge to compete, and thus could consider others' proposals, ask intelligent questions, make suggestions, and enjoy and admire others' work.

I examined the relationship of today's media with the "media" of historical communities, namely, artworks in churches. I discussed why popular movies deserve and need critical attention. Movies articulate and circulate values to a broad audience as religious paintings once did, but do no longer. Religious paintings in museums are not the contemporary equivalent of historical paintings in churches. Because they are removed from the religious context in which they have meaning, they do not act on the viewer religiously. Sixteenth-century Protestant iconoclasts destroyed images because there were no museums in which to place them. By the eighteenth century, iconoclasts simply moved paintings out of churches and into museums, thus disempowering them.

My lecture was a work-in-progress, a good moment in which to receive and consider suggestions. Usually, by the time a scholar gives a lecture, it is well researched and organized and suggestions are not very welcome; they *feel* to the lecturer like criticism. I realized from this experience that scholars should more frequently offer our lectures as *proposals stimulating conversation* rather than as completed works. Lectures could

---

56. Neither has women's ordination been allowed despite a scarcity of male vocations to the priesthood.

be more like Socrates' dialectical explorations than like Aristotle's finished essays. Socrates explored a topic with his friends, asking questions and exploring participants' assumptions, or "silent thoughts." Plato was content, for example, to conclude his only treatise on beauty, not with a definition of beauty, but by acknowledging that "the beautiful things are difficult."[57]

An Aristotelian essay works differently; the author knows the conclusion before he begins; he outlines the steps it will take to demonstrate his thesis; beginning with an *arche*, or starting point, he covers the ground necessary to demonstrate the elegance and accuracy of his conclusion. Most lectures are Aristotelian essays. Scholars seldom make ourselves vulnerable to exploring a topic with an audience. We feel the need to showcase our expertise. Socrates didn't.

---

57. Plato, *Greater Hippias*, 304e.

Chapter 5

Administration, 1996 to 2002

I WAS ON SABBATICAL for the academic year 1994–1995. During that year (including a summer on either end), Owen and I rented a house next to the beach in the little California town of Bolinas so that I could become acquainted with my eight-year-old granddaughter. Siduri and I collected beach glass, smoothed by the waves, to make candleholders; we laboriously decorated Ukranian Easter eggs, and we cooked. One day she ran to the house from the beach to tell me that I must come to see a seal that was "deconstructing on the beach!" I also wrote two books, *Reading for Life* and *Seeing and Believing*.

Meanwhile, the Graduate Theological Union, Berkeley (hereafter GTU) was searching for a Dean. When a member of the search committee called to ask me to comment on a candidate, I realized that *I* would like the position! I was offered and accepted the position of Dean at the GTU, where I had earned my doctorate in 1977. Owen had retired, and by the beginning of the following academic year, 1996–97, we had moved from Cambridge to Berkeley. Moving to the West Coast brought both of us closer to family; Owen also had sons on the West coast. The move was not a good career move for me, but it was a great life move—a choice one sometimes needs to make.

Several publications I had written before coming to Berkeley appeared shortly after I arrived. I struggled to finish several others while fully occupied by learning to be a Dean. My colleagues at GTU seemed to think that it was fine for me to continue to publish, but that is not why I was hired! As in my youth when, for various reasons, I sneaked studying, I now sneaked writing! The early hours of the morning had been "prime time" for writing for me for many years, and I continued to rise early and spend two or three hours writing. However, after about a month of this schedule, I got sick. This told me, "in no uncertain terms," as my father would say, that I could not get up to write at 5:00 a.m., go to my GTU office by 9:00, and maintain a long day of learning, stress, and "people problems." I missed quiet hours of thinking and writing, but the new learning and new people were also exciting.

Seeing and Believing: Religion and Values in the Movies, 1996

This book built on classes I had taught at Harvard Divinity School and earlier projects I have described. In *Seeing and Believing*, I developed a method for analyzing the values communicated in popular movies. I examined the 1980s movies that were most successful at the box office, not art films seen by few people. Having done so I quickly lost interest in movies. Even movies advertised as displaying daring "new" situations were formulaic. Box office success, the bottom line of film production, requires inclusion of titillating scenes—scenes titillating to teenage boys, the audience that determines the box office success of a movie.

First I taught the course. Upper division undergraduates were allowed to take graduate lecture courses; over four hundred student enrolled. I had fourteen teaching fellows to lead discussion sections. The course was listed in the Study of Religion (Harvard University, rather than as an HDS course), so it was well funded. I suspect that many students enrolled because they thought the course would let them watch movies and talk about them; in short, they thought the course would be—in the parlance of 90s undergraduates—a "gut." I lectured once a week, after they had seen the assigned movie, raising critical questions relating to the values represented in the movie. The teaching fellows did the main job of making sure students read and discussed both the movie of the week and the critical theory I had assigned. I told the class that it didn't matter whether I "liked" the movie or not, but as I left the large lecture hall at the end of class among the students, I heard murmurings, "she liked it," or "she didn't like it."

Recollections and Reconsiderations

"Carnal Abominations: The Female Body as Grotesque," *The Grotesque in Art and Literature*, 1997

After many years of noticing misogyny in the history of Christianity, I discovered an underlying strata of male fear and hatred of women's bodies. Simultaneously attracted and repulsed, men often pictured women's bodies as grotesque in the art and literature of the Christian West. The "grotesque" is defined as familiar, yet shockingly alien, permeable, leaking, uncontrollable, weak, and defective in body, mind, and morals. Women were frequently described not only as inferior, but also as evil—daughters of Eve, the prototypical woman who introduced sin into the world. The figure "woman" was usually discussed in pairs, the good woman (obedient, closed and enclosed, like the Blessed Virgin Mary), and the evil woman talkative, open, and curious, like Eve). Actual women were given an image to emulate and an image to avoid. I said to myself, I would like to write a happy book, but if I am to write a happy book I can't continue to write about women!

Reading for Life: Beauty, Pluralism, and Responsibility, 1997

In this book I addressed the issue that remains high on my list of concerns, namely: Is it possible to read simultaneously *both* critically *and* sympathetically? My answer is "reading for life." Reading for life is different than reading for entertainment. It is also different than reading to understand the author's communication. It is not academic reading, assigned reading. Reading for life desperately seeks suggestions—clues—about how to get what I most deeply long for. What behaviors are likely to produce the outcome I desire? In novels readers watch characters acting in ways that either preclude or produce desired results, suggestions that can help us to shape our own behavior. What values direct characters' yearnings? As we read for life, we make silent (often unconscious) judgments for our own lives about the usefulness and potential of characters' values and behavior. We imaginatively construct a *chosen* self.

I suggested that it is often necessary to appropriate advice given by an author that was not intended for a female reader. My example was Rilke's *Letters to a Young Poet*, which, when I was in my twenties, was both influential and inspirational for me. Yet I understood that Rilke's advice was not intended for *me*; I was not the young (male) poet; indeed, the text positioned me to play the part either of "the maid" or the mother, providing unconditional support for the hero. Nevertheless I needed—and appropriated—the book's transformative potential, its encouragement, to develop my own solitude and ambition.

Reading for Life addresses the relationship of beauty and responsibility in a pluralistic society. The book gathers from selected texts a *practical* understanding of the value of beauty within a rich, unpredictable, and strongly pressured human life. To the ancient question, How should we live? my answer is deceptively simple: with enjoyment and generosity. I do not attempt to define beauty. As discussed above, Plato's only treatise on beauty got no further than "the beautiful things are difficult."[1] Beauty cannot be defined; it must be *recognized* by a certain *physical* response:

> There must be those who see this beauty by that with which the soul sees things of this sort, and when they see it they must be delighted and overwhelmed and excited . . . . These experiences must occur whenever there is contact with any sort of beautiful thing, wonder, and a shock of delight and longing and passion and a happy excitement . . . you feel like this when you see in yourself or in someone else greatness of soul, a righteous life, a pure morality, courage . . . he who sees them cannot say anything but that they are what exists. What does "really exist" mean? That they exist as beauties.[2]

Most of the literature I discussed offered insightful proposals, but books also provide cautionary tales. Leni Riefenstahl's *A Memoir* is an exercise in self-justification, a cautionary tale. Riefenstahl, known to history as "Hitler's filmmaker," was undeniably a superb artist and filmmaker. Yet she was unwilling to examine her actions in relation to her social and political circumstances; in the context of World War II and Hitler's agenda, she never acknowledged any wrongdoing. She claimed that she "never for even an instant thought of propaganda."

Citing preoccupation with beauty, Riefenstahl excuses herself from moral responsibility. Clearly *intention* is not sufficient; others immediately understood her to support National Socialism. Actions inevitably entail not only intentions but effects, and inattention cannot excuse blindness to the

---

1. Plato, *Greater Hippias*, 304c.
2. Plotinus, *Ennead*, 1.6.4.

effects of one's work. Pursuing one's passions without *endeavoring* to foresee their effects is irresponsible and morally culpable.³

The practice of reading for life continues to engage me. I contributed an essay to a 2011 volume in honor of the New Testament scholar, Mary Ann Tolbert. "Getting Over Oneself" begins with claims made by historian Lynn Hunt in her book, *Inventing Human Rights*. Hunt demonstrates a *connection* between reformed sensibilities, due largely to the popularity of eighteenth-century epistolary novels, and reformed punishment practices in Europe. Novels enabled readers to empathize with the pain of individuals with whom they were not acquainted, especially impoverished and abused young women. Educated emotions led to altered social sensitivities and practices. Enabled to *imagine* others' pain, populations no longer were *entertained* by public torture and executions.

Several late-twentieth century articles demonstrated and extended my critical approach to contemporary popular culture.

"Larry Flynt in Real Life," *The Christian Century*, 1997

The article reviews a film, "The People vrs. Larry Flynt," directed by Miloš Foreman. The movie depicts the real-life trial of a pornographer, Larry Flynt, publisher of *Hustler* magazine. The suit against Flynt was brought by a mother whose twelve-year-old daughter's strangled body was found next to a copy of *Hustler*. In the trial Flynt insisted on his constitutional right to produce pornography, political satire, and images of violence against women. The Supreme Court decided that Flynt's pornography was constitutionally protected. Fascinated by the "oddities flourishing in American democracy," Foreman's movie sides with the pornographer's "rights" against the "self-righteous uptightness" of his opponents. The film portrays Larry Flynt as a hero fighting for his rights.

My review argues that the film should not be interpreted solely in terms of its agenda of protecting First Amendment rights. Rather it should be considered in relation to American society. The United States Bureau of Justice gives statistics on violence against women in "real life." In 2016 the following statistics were reported on the Bureau's web site:

- 91% of rape victims are women; one in five women will be raped in her lifetime

---

3. Miles, *Reading*, 186.

- 9% of rape victims are men; one in 71 men is victimized
- rape costs the U.S. more than any other crime: $127 billion a year
- rape is the most under reported crime in the U.S.; 63% of rapes are not reported.

It is in *this* context that violent pornography should be understood. If there is any evidence that pornography prompts or encourages violence against women—and there is—it should not be popularly accessible at every newsstand in America.

"What You See is What You Get," *Religion and Prime Time Television*, Michael Suman, ed., 1997

As Marshall McLuhan observed, "We don't see things the way they are. We see things the way we are." According to reports from the Pew Research Center, Americans are becoming more religious, but in different configurations than formerly. America is no longer a three-religion country (Protestant, Roman Catholic, Jewish); religion in America is rapidly becoming more diverse. Only 9 percent of Americans claimed no religion.

Do movies and television reflect the diversity of American religious life? What *kind* of religion is depicted in movies and television? A broad audience can only be expected to watch religion that is either news or entertainment. Either of these categories requires the unusual, dramatic action rather than quiet engagement. Clearly, depictions of religions create a challenge for media. If "religion is what you do with your solitude," as nineteenth-century English Archbishop William Temple said, it is difficult—if not impossible—for media to portray anything but religions' most external (and sensational) moments.

Moreover, media reduces the complexity of religion. For example, the word "Christian" is regularly used in media to refer to the Christian Right. And, since right-wing Christians present their causes in public communication more frequently and effectively than do liberal Christians, the word "Christian" has come to mean what media mean by it.

Recollections and Reconsiderations

"Becoming Answerable for What We See," *Journal of the American Academy of Religion*, 1999 AAR Presidential Address

In my presidential address to the 1999 Annual Meeting of the American Academy of Religion I attempted to resolve an old argument about the difference between "Theological Studies" and the "Study of Religion."[4] Using the ambiguous term "Religious Studies" for both, I said that Religious Studies must practice *both* critical and appreciative scholarship. In the academy, we *study*—we do not *teach*—religion. I explained this important distinction many times to the "cultured despisers" of religion at Harvard University.[5] Teaching religion is done at churches, mosques, and temples, Moreover, in the academy religions must be studied not only for the beauty of their beliefs, liturgies, and practices, but also for the damages they have done and caused, for their *effects*, not only for their intentions. Religious Studies is *inherently* interdisciplinary; it is, irreducibly, the study of the cultures that form religions. Few features of culture are irrelevant to the values and practices of religion—and vice versa.

Anticipating this lecture, I was frightened. I overestimated its importance to the approximately ten thousand members of the American Academy of Religion, many of whom do not attend, but might run their eye over its published version in the *JAAR*. A week or so before I delivered it, I expressed to my father on the phone my feeling of inadequacy to the task. He replied, "I think you're right. You probably shouldn't be doing it." Perversely, I made up my mind to prove him wrong; I had no more feelings of inadequacy. Unintentionally, he had said precisely the right thing!

---

4. I suspect, however, that the argument is not so easily reconciled. It is *fun* to argue about it, and the issue has been a staple of American Academy of Religion conversation for many years.

5. Ironic, since the Divinity School *was* the university in its origins. Harvard existed so that New England could enjoy a "learned ministry." The Divinity School became a graduate school *of* the university in 1816 and celebrated its bicentennial in 2017.

Administration, 1996 to 2002

Plotinus on Body and Beauty: Society, Philosophy, and Religion in Third-Century Rome, 1999

All opposites are entwined together.[6]

Rereading *Plotinus on Body and Beauty*, I found it difficult—sometimes impossible—to maintain critical distance. Again and again I became engulfed in the beauty of Plotinus's universe and sympathetic with his frustration with the inadequacy of language to describe his vision. Plotinus, it seems, would dispute Wittgenstein's maxim, "Anything that can be said can be said clearly."[7] Plotinus's prose became especially tortured when he tried to describe the entities at the top (as it were) and the ground (as it were) of the universe, the One and matter.[8] For example, he says that matter is nonexistent, but immediately adds that "matter has a certain kind of existence."[9]

In the years since its publication I have frequently reread parts of *Plotinus on Body and Beauty*. As Augustine reread his *Confessions* for pleasure and inspiration, I reread *Plotinus on Body and Beauty*. I studied Plotinus originally because Augustine learned from and admired him. Later I studied him for the beauty of his vision. On a sabbatical at the wonderful Rockefeller Study and Conference Center in Bellagio, Italy, I read the *Enneads* in Greek, Plotinus's language. Because Plotinus had impaired physical vision he did not read or edit his original draft, thus giving his reader his unrevised thought. Fortunately, Plotinus was an orderly thinker with enviable powers of concentration.[10] His student and friend, Porphyry, wrote:

> He worked out his train of thought from beginning to end in his own mind, and then, when he wrote it down, since he had set it all in order in his mind, he wrote as continuously as if he were copying from a book. Even if he were talking with someone, engaged in continuous conversation, he kept to his train of thought. He could take his necessary part in the conversation to the full, and at the same time keep his mind fixed without a break on what he was

---

6. Plotinus, *Ennead*, 3.3.6.
7. Ludwig Wittgenstein, *Tractus Logico Philosophicus*, 4.116.
8. Plotinus, *Ennead*, 5.5.6
9. Miles, *Plotinus*, 97.
10. Unlike Plotinus, I must consider my first drafts just that—a first draft. I describe my writing projects as comprised of (at least) two steps: first I write it *down*, then I write it *up*, and the second step usually requires several revisions. Very often I wrote an article in which I thought through a topic before I wrote a book.

considering. When the person he had been talking to was gone, he did not go over what he had written. . . He went straight on with what came next, just as if there had been no interval of conversation between.[11]

I am an historian, not a philosopher, but I believe that historians *should* interpret philosophers. Philosophical approaches often neglect the immediate context and circumstances of a philosopher's thought, seeming to assume that ideas pass from one mind to another, adjusted slightly by each. They often trace ideas from Plato forward, thus losing much of the excitement and all of the immediacy with which they were discussed, whether in the thinker's inner dialogue or with critical friends. In *Plotinus on Body and Beauty*, I sought to demonstrate that recovering ideas "in the life" requires the interests and skills of an historian who endeavors to reconstruct the events, circumstances, and conversations in which the philosopher's ideas were shaped and refined.

Like Augustine's writings, Plotinus's philosophy has been caricatured as dualistic, hierarchical, body-hating, and sex averse.[12] These accusations are no more accurate of Plotinus than they are of Augustine. It is ironic that both authors struggled to overcome precisely these philosophical oversimplifications, but like Porphyry,[13] their popularizers noticed only the *problems* they addressed, not their efforts to resolve them.

Porphyry arranged Plotinus's treatises according to their subjects, but he also listed them chronologically. One of my readings of the *Enneads* was a chronological reading. I sought to understand Plotinus's interests in relation to his age and the events of his life as described by Porphyry. Reading the *Enneads* chronologically produced interesting results. For example, he wrote most appreciatively of death in the last treatise he wrote (1.7), as his body was losing its grip on life.

Plotinus analyzed human beings as composites of body and soul. He did not think of soul as a kind of body, *a location*, but as a *property*, an activity, *life*.[14] Soul *is* life. "Soul vivifies and sensitizes whole bodies and each

---

11. Porphyry, *Life*, 8.

12. "Neoplatonism" is a label ascribed to Plotinus in the seventeenth century. Plotinus thought of himself simply as a faithful follower of Plato.

13. Porphyry's *Life* begins with a statement Plotinus would not have approved, stating that Plotinus was "ashamed of being in a body"; see *Enneads* 2.9.17 for Plotinus's view of body.

14. Miles, *Plotinus*, 58–59.

part of body, a role it could not play if it *were* body."¹⁵ He applied the same method, an apophatic method, in his description of the One—which is without qualities and beyond description—that he used to describe matter. Matter, he wrote, like the One "is apprehended by a process of reasoning which does not come from mind but *works emptily.*"¹⁶ Undaunted by this confusing proposal, Plotinus invokes a default position: Obscurity is beneficial. Heraclitus, he said, taught in riddles, leaving the reader to puzzle out his meaning, because *"we ought to seek for ourselves, as he himself sought and found."*¹⁷

Plotinus acknowledged the existence of "bad men" (ἄνθρωπος κακὸς), presumably made so by bad choices.¹⁸ But do "bad choices" make "bad men"? It seems inconsistent, in Plotinus's universe, to say that people are defined by their choices rather than by their source in the One? Is Plotinus speaking carelessly here? *Hoion?* In any case, "In the bad," he wrote, "life limps."¹⁹

Plotinus's apparently cavalier views of "winners and losers" reflects the entertainment culture in which he lived. The world is like a stadium, he said, in which "some win and others lose."²⁰ Even a highly individual thinker like Plotinus is influenced by the culture in which he lives. Although, according to Porphyry, he practiced charity to individuals, he did not advocate seeking to alter the injustice of his society.

I attempted to reconcile Porphyry's information about Plotinus's engagement with needy others with his apparent indifference to the fact that life generates "winners and losers," unequally endowed individuals. I explained his attitude as commitment to the life of the universe, not primarily to individuals. But commitments to the All and to Intellect are—or seem to be—abstract. On one level, abstract commitments often do not appear to require ethical behavior; indeed, they are often cited to excuse unethical behavior.²¹ However, Plotinus's personal actions certainly indicate concrete commitments, namely, care and protection of *particular* vulnerable persons

---

15. Miles, *Plotinus*, 59–60.
16. Plotinus, *Ennead*, 2.4.12.
17. Miles, *Plotinus*, 67.
18. Plotinus, *Ennead*, 1.1.7.
19. Plotinus, *Ennead*, 1.7.3.
20. Plotinus, *Ennead*, 2.9.9.
21. Perhaps Augustine's "love, and do as you will," is an example; *Homilies on the First Epistle of John*, 7.8.

(widows and orphans). Perhaps his philosophy did not tell everything he knew?[22] Finally, his attitude seems to be that "having done whatever one can do to alleviate suffering, one should accept with equanimity the inequality of life."[23]

Societies like Rome in the third century (Plotinus) and fourth-fifth century (Augustine) that rely heavily on slave labor and entertainment harm the moral sensibility of all their members. Like Plotinus, Augustine tolerated inequality in the family and slavery in the society.[24] In this, American society is not dissimilar to Roman society. American society values entertainment, as can readily be documented by the salaries of sports players and entertainers. Our society also tolerates (and depends on) more or less invisible slavery. In 2016 the U.S. Census Bureau reported approximately 57,000 slaves in America. The bureau defines as slaves persons brought into the Unites States with promises of freedom and wealth, kept under the absolute authority of a "boss," and unable to leave his jurisdiction under threat that family in the slave's country of origin will be harmed if the slave complains or attempts to leave. Moreover, "entertainment" and slavery work together in America. The largest single event requiring slaves—from sex workers to restaurant and hotel workers—is the Super Bowl game.[25]

Plotinus endeavored with "eager longing" to experience the One. Porphyry reports that he achieved this experience on four occasions. Plotinus's frustration with language is at its most intense in his effort to communicate his experience of "rest in the divine."

> But we in our travail do not know what we ought to say, and are speaking of what cannot be spoken, and give it a name because we want to indicate it to ourselves as best we can. But perhaps this name "One" contains only a denial of multiplicity.[26]

---

22. See my further discussion of winners and losers; *Plotinus*, 166.

23. Miles, *Plotinus*, 102.

24. Augustine, *City of God*, XIX 15–19.

25. We usually ignore the fact that the most admired societies in the history of the world would not have survived without slave labor. In societies like our own which do not acknowledge the existence of slaves, who does the slave labor? We must ask also, who benefits? In 2016 the United States Census Bureau estimated 45.8 million slaves in the world. 57,700 slaves are in the United States, 30% more than in 2014; www.U.S.Census Bureau.org.

26. Plotinus, *Ennead*, 5.5.6.

"Rest" is the only word he found to characterize—not the One, but the *experience*. He used the image of a choir to explain:

> We are always around it but do not always look to it; it is like a choral dance: in the order of its singing the choir keeps round the conductor but may sometimes turn away, so that he is out of their sight, but when it turns back to him it sings beautifully and is truly with him; so we too are always around him—and if we were not, we should be totally dissolved and no longer exist—but are not always turned to him; but when we do look to him, then we are at our goal and at rest and do not sing out of tune as we truly dance our god-inspired dance around him.[27]

The last chapter of *Plotinus on Body and Beauty* undertakes to describe Plotinus's potential contribution to present-day quandaries. This is dangerous territory for an historian, especially because "the present" changes between the moment of writing and the publication of a book. The first of these contributions I cited is his orientation to the universe, an orientation lacking in many Americans' secular worldview.

I wrote: if Plotinus's philosophy is to be useful to twenty-first-century people, "we must be prepared to strengthen his sense of the interdependence of body and soul while *we accept his distinction*."[28] It is no longer clear to me that we must accept the substantive distinction of body and soul so evident and fundamental to Plotinus. In *Beyond the Centaur: Imagining the Intelligent Body*, I discussed the harm to philosophy and theology inherent in this distinction (which, by Descartes—not before—became a separation). The intelligent body names a single entity. In fact, Plotinus's whole philosophy depends on his belief that every living being has its source in the One. From the One, through Intellect, through Soul, to the many individuals that participate in the one soul, Plotinus asserts the essential unity of all beings.[29] It is possible to *distinguish* between various activities, but this conceptual act has proved impossible for less subtle thinkers who reify *activities* as *entities*. Yet the very authors most frequently accused of "dualism," Plato and Plotinus, insisted that the distinction between soul and body is a *conceptual* distinction; *it does not exist in reality*.

---

27. Plotinus, *Ennead*, 6.9.8; 4.8.1; 6.9.11.

28. Miles, *Plotinus*, 162.

29. I briefly adopt McKenna's Victorian capitalization of the hypostases here to emphasize *distinctions*, although I usually find that capitalizing the hypotheses leads to thinking of them as *separate entities*.

The second contribution Plotinus can make to contemporary society is to provide a moral compass coordinated to, and reflecting, orientation to the universe. Historically, religions have supplied this orientation, but in doing so they appeal to supernatural divinities. Plotinus did not call upon divinities to confirm his vision of the universe; he sought only to "imagine the real."

Plotinus on Body and Beauty was half written when I moved to the Dean's office at GTU. I struggled to finish the book. But I soon learned that I was no longer able to get up to write in the still-dark early morning hours before beginning my day job as had been my practice throughout my career. Until I retired, I published no book-length projects.

"From the Garden to the Academy: Blame, Battle, or a Better Way?" *Journal of Feminist Studies in Religion*, 2001

This article represents an attempt to *think through* the culture of academic institutions and how it might be changed for the better. After analyzing statistics on the current hiring practices and salaries of women faculty, I made several "modest proposals." My suggestions place a great deal of responsibility on administrators to design conditions in which women faculty can thrive. I was once in the awkward position of arguing against the inclusion of a woman faculty member on a time-consuming committee when I knew that she was trying to finish writing a book so that it could be peer-reviewed before her promotion to tenure was considered. Male faculty have learned that every committee needs a woman member, but I remark cynically that the woman will be less valued for her perspective than because male faculty have noticed that women members actually *do* the committee work, read the applications (even the applicant's book or articles), *and* supply the coffee.

I sought a model somewhere between the traditional model in which several (male) administrators make decisions in secret, requiring mutual confidentiality, and the "scatter-shot" model that women—who have no direct access to decision-making—typically use. I call this model the "modified town meeting." Everyone knows who must eventually make the decision (which is not made at the time of the meeting). The town meeting exposes the issues, allowing those with interests in the decision to speak, so that the decision-maker understands the potential damages and advantages of the decision. After a decision is made, the decision-maker reveals the values, priorities, and commitments that informed her decision.

I undertook several projects whose goal was strengthening GTU. I urged that GTU hire a professor of Islamic Studies, and a professor trained in Women's Studies, rather than continuing to expect that women faculty, trained in other fields, would provide this perspective and expertise. Both of these positions were hired after my tenure as Dean.

Other projects met with greater immediate success. I wrote my first grant proposal for half a million dollars to enable GTU to hire a pioneer in the field of Women's Studies. Rosemary Radford Ruether accepted a term appointment and proved immensely generous and popular. She advised the student group interested in ecological concerns and, in addition to her other classes, she taught a seminar in Spanish on Latin American theology. In the interest of consortium building, I was able to provide funds for several years for faculty groups in several fields across the GTU schools to meet for talk and dinner. I hoped to increase mutual familiarity and trust among the GTU schools. Although faculty in various fields of theological study were trained, not denominationally, but in the same few doctoral programs, the GTU schools each insisted on hiring faculty in traditional fields—like New Testament—rather than sharing faculty across the curriculum. If more faculty sharing were done, I thought, faculty could be hired in less traditional fields, such as Diversity Studies, Critical Theory, or Cultural Studies.

Consortium building was my primary agenda. The GTU schools already shared a common library, cross registration within a common course curriculum, and classrooms. I urged that sharing be extended to faculty and a common chapel. However, boards of the schools were not primarily interested in consortium building, but rather in the education of future denominational clergy. School boards seemed to fear that faculty sharing would cause the schools to lose their denominational distinctiveness. I tried, largely unsuccessfully, to convince school presidents that a stronger consortium would not mean weaker schools.

Ultimately, however, I was disappointed in what I could accomplish as a Dean. I had thought that a relatively new institution—the forty-year-old Graduate Theological Union—would be more responsive to change than the three-hundred-and-fifty-plus-year-old university from which I came. I learned, however, that institutional change is not likely to occur within a five-year appointment. I left the office recommending that the Dean's role should circulate among faculty members for five-year appointments—long enough to develop awareness of, and sympathy for, the limitations with which a Dean must work, but not long enough for a faculty member to lose touch with the current conversation in her/his field. I advised against "career deans," which strengthen antagonisms between faculty and administration.

Perhaps the short length—five years—of my tenure in the Dean's office says it all. I found that administration was not my first love in the academy. Nor was I temperamentally well suited to it. Born administrators, I think, do not spend night hours worrying about the many decisions a Dean must make. Nevertheless, I learned a great deal in my years as Dean, and I am grateful for the experience.

PART III

Chapter 6

Retirement Part I, 2002 to 2011

AFTER I RETIRED IN 2001 from my appointment as Dean, my publications increased. I spent the next year (until I became sixty-five) teaching. I recalled what I loved most about academic life, namely, students and the classroom. While I was Dean I taught one course each term, but these were courses that did not require much preparation, courses I had taught many times. In 2001–2002, I realized that I did not know how to teach graduate students on the West Coast effectively. Harvard students enjoyed a well-crafted lecture, but GTU students wanted to talk. The assigned readings were in historical texts (in translation), but historical "background" and "context" were needed. I needed to sketch for students the conversation in which the text we read was one voice. So I gave short lectures, and more and more classroom time was spent in discussions.

"Bonhoeffer (the Film) and Bonhoeffer (the Theologian)," a review of the documentary film *Bonhoeffer* (2003) directed by Martin Doblmeier, AAR presentation, 2004

Deitrich Bonhoeffer was a Christian theologian in Nazi Germany. Son of a prosperous middle-class family, he ignored the treatment of Jews in Germany until he taught for a time in New York City's "Hell's Kitchen," where he became aware of the suffering of African Americans. Sensitized to human suffering, he returned to Germany where he noticed the persecution of German Jews. As he worked to reverse the German Church's apparent indifference to Nazi treatment of Jews, he became part of a group plotting to assassinate Hitler. A suitcase bomb, placed in a meeting Hitler attended, exploded, killing several men—but not Hitler. Bonhoeffer was arrested, imprisoned, and executed.

I wrote: "The film offers a case study in a complex human situation, inviting its viewer to recognize that we all, always, must somehow act with conviction in the dark, in uncertainty. We do not know what is generously responsible in particular situations. We understand even our own intentions with limited clarity. We pursue the human good without assurances of its realization. Because of the difficulty and discomfort of living with such ambiguity, we design principles to provide us with guidance that we hope will limit the damages of our actions. But finally, whether we recognize and acknowledge it or not, like Bonhoeffer we *all, whether we are religious or not*, live by faith.

Moreover, instead of seeking assurance that we are "doing the right thing," I have learned to substitute the twentieth-century British philosopher R. G. Collingwood's definition of "duty": "that which I, and only I, can do in this, and only this, situation." Collingwood's idea of duty requires both an accurate understanding of the circumstance in which I find myself, and self-knowledge.

"Achieving the Christian Body: Visual Incentives to Imitation of Christ in the Christian West," 2004

This article continues the theme of my 1994 article, "Imitation of Christ: Is It Possible in the Twentieth Century?" The earlier article explored historical devotional texts that advocate imitation of Christ; this article considers the visual images that urged and supported imitation of Christ.

While images are usually considered illustrations of texts, this is not true of all images. My Harvard Divinity School course, "Images in Historical Theology," considered visual images as primary texts; literary texts "illuminated" the images, articulating the ideas that inspired and informed them. Images often offer alternative interpretations of texts. For example, St. Paul's use of "flesh" as symptom and symbol of original sin prompted devotional texts to adopt this meaning literally; but visual images throughout the history of Christianity revealed the centrality of "flesh" in Christian belief and practice. The article provides rich detail demonstrating the importance of visual texts to Christian practice.

"Sex and the City (of God): Is Sex Forfeited or Fulfilled in Augustine's Resurrection of Body?" *Journal of the American Academy of Religion*, 2005

In the twenty-first century, as in the first century, the resurrection of body is an article of faith for Christians. In more than two thousand years since the earliest Christians, no progress has been made in rendering the doctrine of bodily resurrection credible. Yet lack of evidence has not prevented Christians from speculating about resurrected bodies and their environment, heaven. From Augustine's extended fantasy in the last book of *The City of God* to contemporary fundamentalists' anticipation of white robes, harps, and golden streets, imagining the resurrection of body has been a tempting topic. Augustine, the doctrine's most articulate historical proponent, seems to exclude sex (as we knew it) from resurrected bodies.[1] Nevertheless, it is difficult to imagine "real bodies"—as Augustine insisted—that lack this most intimate and pleasurable capacity of bodies.

Let us lay aside, for the moment, Augustine's reputation for body-denying, sex-aversive, and "dualistic" commitments. This common misunderstanding of Augustine cannot explain why he seems to have excluded so integral and pleasurable a feature from resurrection bodies. Neither does his own sexual experience, as reported long after the fact in his *Confessions*, adequately answer the question about why he omitted this greatest human pleasure (*summa voluptas*) from resurrection rewards. In this article I first summarized the twenty-first-century discourse about sexuality emerging from Freud and his critics in order begin to understand the differences that must be taken into account between contemporary discourse surrounding sexuality and Augustine's understanding.

I conclude that Augustine neither explicitly included nor excluded "sexuality,"[2] but that a "post-Augustinian" proposal about "heavenly sex" can be hazarded based on Augustine's suggestions. A key to Augustine's values is whether a feature of human experience surfaces in his imagined resurrection body, and he includes biological sex—men's and women's bodies—in resurrected bodies, but not (genital) sex acts. Because death will not exist in the resurrection, sex will not be needed to reproduce the human race. Nevertheless, "beauty, pleasure, wonder, amazement, and loveliness"

---

1. Even Thomas Aquinas, who asserted that all the senses will be incrementally more sensitive in resurrected bodies, does not picture sex as a heavenly pastime.

2. A modern term referring to Freud's understanding of the discourse surrounding and defining sexual objects and goals.

will be present in the *distributed* sexuality of resurrected bodies. No longer defined by genitally organized activity, a "sexuality of eternally blissful sensuality," a sensuality in which the urgency associated with object and *goal*—that is, sex "as we knew it"—has disappeared, but pleasure remains and is enhanced.

The Word Made Flesh: A History of Christian Thought, 2005

My only textbook emerged from the course I taught many times at Harvard Divinity School and once at the Graduate Theological Union, "History of Christian Thought." *The Word Made Flesh* discusses "the beauty and the tragic harms done in the name of Christianity" from the end of the first century to the beginning of modernity, defined by the spread of "enlightenment" at the end of the eighteenth century.

After I retired I wrote "up" my twenty years of lectures in "History of Christian Thought." Over the years I had "written down" lecture notes, some more developed than others, but until I retired and no longer taught the course, I did not publish my lectures because I did not know what else I would say in class if students could simply read my lectures.[3] The course was always large enough to have discussion sections, but too large to discuss primary texts in the class. It was important to consider texts in their historical circumstances, so my lectures endeavored to supply context.

My article, "Tasteless Historical Stories: An Historical Theologian's Responsibility to Past and Present" (2005), a preamble to *The Word Made Flesh*, describes my historical method. It contains an argument for using the literature, music, images, liturgies, and practices of the Christian movement as primary evidence. *The Word Made Flesh* also discusses dissenters, debates, and alternative interpretations. From the perspective of the "winners" of Christian history, these views were called "heretical" understandings of Christianity, escalating the "merely different" into the "absolutely other."[4]

The Word Made Flesh seeks to communicate a vivid sense of the *life* of historical people who lived and died as Christians. It offers a history of diversity, a recovery of the rich pluralism *within* Christianity. What I called

---

3. In fact, one year an entrepreneurial student recorded, transcribed, and sold copies of my lectures!

4. Young, *Justice*, 98.

"tasteless historical stories" break into and frequently undermine the traditional seamless triumphal story, told by church historians, of the growth and development of Christianity. A cohesive story of such an immense and varied movement should not be told as incremental "development." *The Word Made Flesh* is both sympathetic, reveling in the beauty of Christian movements, and critical, noticing their many abuses.

How was Christianity, a new religion in the early centuries of the common era, to gain recognition in societies that did not value new religions? The early apologists sought to establish Christianity in the cultural niche occupied by ancient philosophies, that is, as a response to the question, How should we live? They represented Christianity as an alternative to established religions and philosophies. By the fourth century and for many centuries thereafter, Christian belief was strongly associated with intellectual assent to creedal statements.

Fourth-century ecumenical—empire-wide, authoritative—councils were devoted to precision in beliefs. The sad result of creeds defined by church councils was that large groups of Christians found that councils' definitions—of Christ's divinity and humanity and other matters—were not what they envisioned when they prayed. Fifty years after the 451 CE Council of Chalcedon, three major churches separated because they differed from authorized beliefs; by 600 CE "the Monophysite empire was vast, geographically much greater than that of the Latin and Orthodox churches combined." Nestorians, Manichaeans, and Jacobites also formed their own churches.[5]

The history of these non-Chalcedonian churches lies largely outside the Roman Empire. To access their history, languages other than Greek and Latin are needed! When I was a doctoral student in the early 1970s, it was assumed that knowledge of Latin and Greek would give access to the literature of early Christianity. But knowledge of Greek and Latin keeps historians of my generation focused on the Mediterranean. If I were starting again I would learn Slavic languages, Armenian, and Coptic—as several contemporary scholars do—thus incrementally increasing knowledge of the wealth of world Christianity.[6] *The Word Made Flesh* can only suggest this richness, omitting—as I, being linguistically challenged, must—Christianity as it developed worldwide.

---

5. Appeals to Christian "unity" are further discussed in chapter 9, 177ff.

6. A sobering thought: if Augustine had written in Punic I would know nothing about his thinking!

Recollections and Reconsiderations

"The Passion for Social Justice and *The Passion of the Christ*," Mel Gibson's Bible: Religion, Popular Culture, and The Passion of the Christ, 2006

My review of Mel Gibson's movie, *The Passion of the Christ*, states the obvious: the movie is violent entertainment. "The medium is the message," as Marshall McLuhan observed. Its box office appeal is amply demonstrated; it amassed $370 million in the nineteen weeks it appeared on the top-ten list.

Gibson reported that he wanted to produce a movie "faithful to the gospels and Christian belief." As has often been seen, however, authors' intentions do not necessarily guarantee results compatible with intentions. Americans view movies in a position of distance and passivity, eating popcorn; violence is entertainment.

I suggested that "The Passion of the Christ," effectively served as "misdirection," a magician's term for gestures that attract attention away from what he is doing. By focusing on what was *done to* Jesus in his last days, attention is diverted from his ministry, from what *he did*. For Jesus spent his short life not only preaching and teaching, but also healing the sick and feeding the hungry. I provided statistics revealing the urgent need for health care and food for marginalized and vulnerable members of American society. The statistics in the article need to be updated; they would, I think, be even more dramatic than those of a decade ago when the article was published.

Christians could become better Christians, I suggested, not by empathizing with (Gibson's depiction of) Christ's sufferings, but by participating in Christ's teachings and ministry. A present-day imitation of Christ could support social programs that feed the hungry and provide health care. The Christ who drove the money-changers from the temple would also be very likely to protest corporate greed in American society. The active, compassionate Christ of the ministry years has much to teach American society. But it is not likely that a movie about *that* Christ would be successful at the box office.

"The Eye of the Beholder," Introduction to *The Subjective Eye: Essays in Culture, Religion, and Gender in Honor of Margaret R. Miles*, 2006.

I am grateful for this *festschrift* in my honor, contributed to by colleagues, friends, and former students. The volume was presented to me at a dinner at the American Academy of Religion 2006 meeting in San Antonio. It was not a surprise, as I had been invited to write the Introduction. The volume, edited by Richard Valantasis (in collaboration with Deborah J. Haynes, James D. Smith, and Janet Carlson), was organized in sections reflecting my academic interests: Historical Theology, Religion and Culture, Religion and Gender, and Religion and the Visual Arts. It was an enormous pleasure to read the essays that involved ideas the authors and I had worked on together, now carried forward to topics I could not have predicted.

Against the traditional assumption that scholarship is lonely, I underscored the importance of collegial work in the Introduction: "Scholars are only as good as the conversations in which they participate." Delight in scholarship, I said, "is contagious. One catches it from warm bodies in a room." This sentence reveals my lack of esteem for distance learning. I also oppose PowerPoint presentations, which, I claim, are training a generation to be unable to comprehend a nuanced argument. PowerPoint invites viewers to notice and remember only the bottom line, the one-sentence on-screen summary. Listening carefully and critically may soon be a lost skill.

After considering the contribution of each essay to Religious Studies, I conclude that scholarship is a luxury and a privilege. I cite a quotation I have enjoyed for many years, quoted in the preface to Suzanne Langer's profoundly serious book, *Philosophy in a New Key*: "All the genuine deep delight in life is in showing people the mud pies you have made: and life is at its best when we confidently recommend our mud pies to each other's sympathetic consideration."[7] I told generations of Harvard students suffering from bad consciences about their undeniable privilege that the appropriate response to privilege is not guilt, but gratitude and responsibility.

---

7. The author is J. M. Thornburn, otherwise unknown to me.

Recollections and Reconsiderations

"Living Lovingly in a Culture of Fear," *I Have Called You Friends: Reflections on Reconciliation in Honor of Frank T. Griswold*, 2006

North American media is powerful—for good or ill. I am frequently tempted to notice only media's deleterious effects, but then I recall its contributions to the common good. For example, the media campaign against smoking has changed our culture. When I was a student, the air in seminar rooms—where students sit for three hours at a time—were blue with smoke. Smokers owned the air everyone breathed. Presently, smokers are required to smoke at a safe distance from other breathers. This amazing change in a relatively short time is due largely to media campaigns that informed all Americans of the dangers of smoking. Together with education in schools, advertisements on billboards and in magazines and newspapers, smoking rates in the United States have plummeted. Media campaigns to inform and warn about a number of threats to individuals and the common good—such as unsafe sex, texting while driving, and unhealthy foods—have also influenced many Americans.

But fear factors sell newspapers. And fear factors fatigue, so new dangers are regularly proposed and exaggerated. As a result, Americans fear the wrong things. Since 2001 terrorism has been a primary fear factor, but in that year, 42,000 Americans were killed in traffic accidents while 3,547 were killed *worldwide* in terrorist attacks, 3000 of them on 9/11. Fear in individuals and societies can be exploited by politicians and commerce. Augustine advocated that the energy of fear be intentionally and deliberately gathered and "carried over" to love.

"Mapping Feminist Histories of Religious Traditions," *Journal of Feminist Studies in Religion*, 2006

This article introduced a roundtable discussion with Virginia Burrus, Tazim R. Kassam, and Rita M. Gross.

When I wrote *The Word Made Flesh* I searched for a history of Christian women that could begin to work toward a gender-inclusive history of Christianity. I realized that the traditional model featuring "development" and "progress" is not a usable frame for an inclusive history. The history of progress and development has been tirelessly written and rewritten without challenging the absence of Christian women who gave birth to—and raised—the male leaders of the Christian movements. To begin to address this problem I proposed three methodological strategies: First, inclusion of historical women when they can be found in evidence; second, reconstruction of women's experience based on the expectations of their societies; third, the absence of women's experience can be noticed. *Why* is the home to which most historical women were confined—the stable ground of historical communities and location of everyone's upbringing—missing, or at best elusive, requiring too much conjecture to be plausible?

I urged historians of women's experience to resist the temptation to identify with historical women who apparently embody the characteristics that twenty-first-century women value, namely, women who are rebels in the context of their societies. Seeking historical women on the basis of current sympathies and sensitivities is "narcissistic and self-referential."[8] Responses from a Christian, a Buddhist, and a Moslem historian of women provide rich suggestions, illuminating the infinitely varied experience of women and the difficulty of recovering it.

"Not Nameless but Unnamed: The Woman Torn from Augustine's Side," *Feminist Interpretations of Augustine*, 2007

Early feminists mined the writings of Augustine, a North African Christian bishop who lived approximately fifteen hundred years ago, for information about his attitude toward, and treatment of, women. Before feminist historians had developed and demonstrated more sophisticated methods for reading and interpreting historical texts, Augustine was invariably condemned in their writings. Although he may not always deserve to be interpreted more favorably by more recent methods, these methods focus more on *understanding* the social and cultural conditions, the assumptions, and the experiences of young men of Augustine's class than on judgments based on translations of his (Latin) writings. Historical *criticism* demonstrates the multiple factors involved in an historical perspective, while *judgment* rushes to conclusions, usually interpreting language (in translation) literally, ignoring complexity.

In this article I offered a critical historical interpretation of Augustine's literary treatment of women and his self-report, primarily in his

---

8. Rogoff, "Tiny Anguished Reflections," 40.

Confessions, of his relationships with actual women. I focused on three of the women who make cameo appearances in the *Confessions*: Augustine's mother, Monnica; his partner of fifteen years and the mother of his son; and the young heiress to whom he was briefly engaged. Each of these women occupied a different social niche in late Roman North African society. I argued that, without using far too much imagination, we cannot reconstruct fully fleshed characters. We can, however, learn a great deal about the conditions and choices available to them from what we know about their social niches. Exploring the social location of each provides information about them that Augustine's text fails to supply. This strategy, I suggested, gives the most promising access to understanding the lives of women who did not record their own lives and thoughts.

"*Facie ad Faciem*: Visuality, Desire, and the Discourse of the Other, *Journal of Religion*, 2007

In this essay I explored a little noticed feature of Plato and Plotinus's theories of vision, namely the *connection* between physical vision and spiritual vision.[9] It both builds on, and corrects, my 1981 article, "Vision, the Eye of the Body and the Eye of the Mind in Saint Augustine's *De trinitate* and *Confessions*." Both physical and spiritual vision are prompted by desire. In Plato's account, spiritual vision ("desire for the invisible") begins with physical vision—"one beautiful body"—and, without rejecting its starting point, advances to noticing beauty in laws, institutions, and ways of life. "Vision is the foundation, ground, energy, and impetus of desire."

Beauty, we often remark, is in the eye of the beholder. The essay explores the origins of this statement that has, in contemporary usage, become a cliché. Like taste, we think of beauty as a nonnegotiable judgment based irrefutably on the personal predilections of the speaker. Plato and Plotinus sought a more objective identification of beauty. They proposed that beauty is recognizable, not by certain identifiable qualities in an *object*, but by a certain *physical* response in its viewer. Beauty produces *physical* effects.

9. A technical problem slowed the preparation of this article. I originally used long quotations in Greek, but I could not find the Greek font on my computer. I spent hours looking for it, and others tried to help. Finally, I asked my computer repairperson how to find it. He replied that he had removed it, reasoning that no one could possibly want a Greek font (taking up space) on the computer! So I translated the Greek passages into English; later I found that the journal in which my article was published did not want long passages in Greek in the essay!

Both Plato and Plotinus describe these effects: "wonder, and a shock of delight, and longing and passion, a happy excitement [and] wild exultation."[10]

Desire is prompted by seeing beauty *at the level of perception*, not by aesthetic judgment. The ability to see *as* beauty is not the automatic result of education or maturity, but the result of a committed and patient effort, a spiritual discipline. To see beauty is to see the object *in its life*, to grasp the connections by which it exists.

Beauty, like ugliness, is in the eye of the beholder. But even ugliness has its particular beauty, as I suggest in the following essay.

"Rouault and the Dynamics of Self-Deception," *Mystic Masque: Semblance and Reality in Georges Rouault*, [exhibition catalog], 2008

This essay began when I was invited to reflect on an artist with whom I was initially unfamiliar. I was able to identify Rouault by his trademark *chiaroscuro*, but I knew nothing further. Studying his paintings closely I recognized that they demonstrate that self-deception and deception of others is a major theme of his paintings. Self-deception *shows* on bodies; it is hard on bodies. Rouault regarded his characters' self-deception and their efforts to deceive others primarily as neither dishonest nor sinful, but as overwhelmingly and profoundly sad. Even Rouault's clowns are sad; their pitiful efforts at humor are quintessential sadness. Rouault's art seeks to show suffering in a way that invites sympathy rather than provides voyeuristic enjoyment of others' pain.

In his quest for the happy life, Augustine learned that suffering is caused by desperately clutching at unfulfilling objects. In his *Confessions* he described the amusements of children and adults; children's interest in "footballs, nuts, and pet sparrows," is succeeded by interest in "business... gold, estates, and slaves." *The objects differ, but the dynamic is the same.* He said that the appropriate attitude toward the unhappiness resulting from self-deception is not judgment but *sympathy*. "And no one is sorry for the children; no one is sorry for the older people; no one is sorry for both of them."[11] Rouault's art depicts suffering that prompts sympathy.

In *Seeing and Believing*, I analyzed scenes from several popular 1980s movies to demonstrate that suffering is often shown from the perspective of

---

10. Plato, *Phaedrus*, 25 1a-e; Plotinus, *Ennead*, 1.6.4, 1.6.5.
11. Augustine, *Confessions*, 1.9.

the triumphant perpetrator, not from that of the victim. Sightlines proceed from the eye of the perpetrator to the suffering victim, inviting the viewer to identify with the assailant's triumph, not with the victim's pain.

Later, in "Augustine and Freud: The Secularization of Self-Deception" (2012), I argued that the distinction between self-deception and optimism can be very difficult to locate with any precision. I suggested that self-deception should not be thought of as a mental activity that is always deleterious. For example, self-deception can enable a person with terminal disease to ignore the imminence of death in order to enjoy a beautiful day. In fact, people who suffer from clinical depression are unable to practice positive self-deception. They find in every happy moment the insidious presence of inevitable pain and death; every joy is disastrously undermined by awareness of the omnipresence of suffering.

"Seeing is Believing: Shinjo Ito and the Role of Vision in Religious Practice," *The Vision and Art of Shinjo Ito* [exhibition catalog], 2008

In 2008 I received an unusual invitation. Three people—a curator and two Shinnyo-en priests—came from Tokyo to invite me to contribute an essay to an exhibition catalog of Buddhist art by the monk and artist, Shinjo Ito, founder of the Shinnyo-en Buddhist order. Until now, this art had not been seen outside the temple for which it was created. Shinjo Ito's sculpture, calligraphy, and photography was now to tour to several venues in North America and Europe. My first reaction was that I was undoubtedly the wrong person to comment on the exhibition. I knew very little about Buddhist art. But my visitors assured me that many Buddhist art experts had been and would be consulted; what they wanted from me was an "outsider eye." They had read my writings on Christian art and liked my "eye." As we talked about their hopes for the exhibition I began to see that I *could* write an essay on the role of vision in religious practice, making some interesting comparisons between Eastern and Western theories of religious art. I agreed, and my visitors returned to Japan.

What do viewers think is happening when they look at religious art? I found points of agreement in Eastern and Western theories of religious vision. Plato described vision as occurring when a quasi-physical ray from the viewer's eye *touches* an object, *connecting* viewer and object. Vedic literature also understood vision as touching its object. The object, in turn, moves back along the visual ray, imprinting itself on the viewer's soul. Modern theories of vision are more physically accurate accounts, but the visual ray is a perfect theory of *religious* vision. Viewer and religious object *connect* and *communicate* as the viewer's visual ray *touches* the religious object.

The book (*Getting Here from There*, with Hiroko Sakomura), published in 2011, originated with this essay. Our friendship began on the day my visitors from Tokyo arrived.

"A Feminine Figure in Christian Tradition," *Conversations: Luce Irigaray*, 2008

The French psychoanalyst and feminist, Luce Irigaray, initiated this conversation between herself, (then) doctoral student Laine Harrington, and me. Irigaray invited our comments on her article, "La rédemption des femmes," which she characterized as "a personal struggle to critically appropriate the meaning of the Incarnation from a Roman Catholic perspective," an effort to better understand her own tradition while avoiding "blind submission."

Harrington and Miles questioned several points of Irigaray's article. We asked her to elaborate on her suggestion that the figure of the (couple) Virgin Mary and the Christ Child carries potential for valorizing both men and women. We did not understand how the male-defined figure of Mary can be liberating. Mary, figure of the ideal woman, is obedient, accommodating, comforting, "enclosed," and nourishing, lacking self-definition or initiative. Apparently dismayed by this observation, Irigaray responded that our response did not contribute to "our way to a feminine spiritual embodiment." She also noted a "Protestant inclination to question tradition" that was at odds with her Roman Catholic approach.

Although largely unrecognized, the broader cultural conversations from which each of us—Irigaray, Harrington, and Miles—spoke largely determined the commitments implicit in our conversation. American religious feminists are influenced by Mary Daly's statement (in *Beyond God the Father*) that if a symbol *can* be used oppressively against women, and in fact *has been used oppressively*, it is not a symbol that can be fruitfully reinterpreted for contemporary feminist use. Centuries-old oppressive meanings have a psychic durability that cannot be summarily overcome when a different interpretation is proposed. Speaking from within French religious feminist conversation, Irigaray thought it possible boldly to appropriate and reinterpret the figure of the BVM for feminist use.

Recollections and Reconsiderations

"[D]ialogue takes place between... different subjects who do not share *a priori* the same truth." Although Irigaray wrote this statement in a different context, her definition of dialogue describes our conversation. Moreover, not only were our "truths" different, but also our values, and more importantly, the conversations in which they were imbricated. Moreover, Irigaray, a psychoanalyst, primarily addressed the use of religious symbols in the service of *individuation*. Significantly, she proposes *breathing* as an alternative to speaking, thus privileging *private* over public meaning. Recognizing that it is possible to construct and use private interpretations of religious symbols, Miles and Herrington foreground *public* interpretations and their effects. Unfortunately we ignored the larger cultural conversations that informed our perspectives, our values, and our interests. Thus the proposed dialogue clarified two differing perspectives, but did not lead to mutual understanding.

A Complex Delight: The Secularization of the Breast, 1350–1750, 2009

Between 1350 and 1750 CE the public meaning of naked breasts changed dramatically. In 1350 many images of the Virgin Mary's exposed breast, offered to the infant Christ, represented God's love for humanity as the provision of life, nourishment, and loving care. By 1750, the female breast was no longer site and symbol of religious subjectivity. Public signification of the breast had changed from a powerful religious symbol to medical and erotic meanings. Breasts were displayed either as "objects to be dissected, studied and drawn" (the medical breast), or in early modern pornography, as the erotic breast. Myriad religious and cultural factors brought about this change. Researching these factors, it became evident that "no firm boundaries between visual 'text' and social 'context' exist." Visual text and social context interacted to create this significant change.

The book sought to demonstrate that "images, carefully interpreted in their historical setting, constitute historical evidence." Images were primary evidence of public interest and interpretation, but once I noticed the images, texts contemporary with the images could be identified. Lacking texts, the interpreter is in danger of projecting her own visual training onto the society she seeks to understand.

> Historians are often tempted to claim assurance in regard to their interpretation that goes beyond the possibility of documentation.

> The more air-tight and self-assured a historian's account, the more readers should be prompted to ask, What is *not* there, and how might different evidence alter the proposed interpretation? . . . [T]he evidence supports my conviction that what I see was really "there," but then, so were many other things that, if taken into account, might alter beyond recognition the pattern I see.[12]

In short, humility is incumbent on historians. All historical accounts are hypotheses. The more persuasive an interpretation is as *story*, the more tentatively the interpretation should be proposed. In fact, the primary method by which a story is created is "data reduction." Reducing the "blooming buzzing" mess of history to a plausible story involves ignoring a great deal of (potential) evidence. Popular historians who deliver a story often do not acknowledge this; the more speculative the historical picture, the more confidently and didactically it is presented. Most historians are not willing to say simply, I have studied this historical situation for many years and this is what I see.

A leitmotiv of *A Complex Delight* is a reevaluation of the common modern assumption that erotic and religious images are necessarily opposite and opposing. The exposed breast of the Virgin Mary questions this assumption, for in late medieval and renaissance images, the breast combines erotic and religious meaning. Reducing "erotic" to genital meaning, modern sensibilities have lost the original meaning of *eros* which, according to the *Lexicon Plotinianum* mingled "carnal desire and nobler motives."[13] *Eros*, the excitement and energy of the intelligent body is undifferentiated. In the early centuries of the common era, the classical *distinction* of body and soul/mind veered toward a separation that became explicit only in Descartes (in the seventeenth century). It was this distinction/separation that fostered the polarization of erotic and religious.

---

12. Miles, *Complex Delight*, 19.
13. *Lexicon Plotinianum*, col. 430.

Chapter 7

Retirement Part II, 2011 to 2017

1

AFTER 2010 MY WRITING became more explicitly autobiographical. I had two reasons for adopting a different writing style and content. First, a practical reason: being retired, I no longer needed to "beef up" my *curriculum vitae*. Second and more importantly, I began to think that "objectivity" masked the fact that the experiences and training of the interpreter inevitably affects—if not directs—both the topics chosen and the interpretation given. Autobiographical elements also appear at more subtle levels. All history has an element of fiction. As discussed in chapter 6, the creation of a recognizable story requires, first and foremost, data reduction, a weeding out of historical evidence that is irrelevant, or contradictory, to the historian's story. Scholarly honesty requires, then, that the historian reveal at least the most relevant elements of her perspective, such as, training in a certain methodology or loyalty to particular ideologies or religious institutions. It is not possible to *omit* perspective; the only alternative is to ignore it, pretending that perspective plays no part in historical interpretation.

Undoubtedly, reflecting on historical evidence *with my life*, with my lived and living experience is a valuable exercise *for me*, but is autobiographical reflection on historical evidence anything more than narcissistic? What prevents it being merely idiosyncratic? Intentions are not enough; I certainly *intend* to be helpful on both personal and social levels, but I cannot control the *effects* of my authorship. But the effects can, to some extent, be anticipated and managed. Experience can be offered as *suggestive*, not presented as "the right way," That is, as absolute or universal. Furthermore, it can describe not *how to think*, but how *I think*. Even Descartes, who has been called the "father of rationalism," insisted that his *Discourse* was *first-personal*.[1] *He* suggested that his *method*, not—or not necessarily—his *conclusions*, might be useful to others.[2]

A further note on method: when a doctrine or an idea perplexed me, I (virtually) pinned it to the front of my mind and left it there. As I went about the business of daily life, I brought everything I experienced to it to see whether any light was shed. Often, a reformulation of the question was necessary; the clarified or expanded question represented a step toward understanding. I was patient; I kept the apparent conundrum in the front of my mind until it yielded either understanding or the next question. This method made my life rich and full of wonder. *The Long Goodbye* illustrates the greater value of *methods* than *conclusions*.

Writing autobiographically involves a different kind of attentiveness than does academic writing. When I had a grief or a problem—an alcoholic son, a brother with mental illness, a husband with dementia —I asked myself whether this was a personal problem or a social problem. Inevitably it was both, so I wrote about it as both, on the one hand hopeful of helping people with similar problems and, on the other hand, seeking to raise public consciousness of the problem and (often) the scarcity of resources available for dealing with it.

My later writings are free of the inescapable urgency of a young academic. In my middle years, I began to recognize that I do not write to satisfy external requirements; nor do I write with hope of changing the world—even the world of scholarship.[3] I write primarily for myself, to *know what*

---

1. "My aim here is not to teach the method that each person should follow in order to conduct his reason well, but solely to show in what way I have conducted my own." He wanted to show "*not what can be known*, but what *I* can know"; Descartes, *Discourse*, 1.2; 1.4. Recall also the latter books of Augustine's *Confessions* in which he sought not to understand the "origin of evil," but what *he* "silently thinks" about time, memory, etc.—and exploration of his own mind.

2. By contrast, in his *Confessions*, Augustine described his youth as a stressful process of chasing objects in the fear that something would be missed. But he made it clear that others should not adopt his *method*. Rather he urged that others accept his *conclusions*.

3. I have endeavored, with very limited success, to rehabilitate Augustine's reputation among educated people. I also attempted, with even less success, to present Plotinus in a more accurate light than the settled prejudice with which he is usually approached.

I think. I have often said that the scholarly life is enormously privileged in that, when I die, I will know what I think on matters of importance to me. I appreciate deeply the opportunity of study and the excitement and energy with which I was gifted.

Like my earlier publications but even more so, I write *Recollections and Reconsiderations* to know what I think. I also want to comprehend my publications as a *corpus*, a body of work directed by my values and commitments—not this, then that, then the next thing. In the midst of a busy professional life, it is often difficult to see why I chose particular subjects, and what seemed to me important to say about them. Tutored by Augustine, I wanted to discern and *spell out* the integrity of my life that, in the stress of its busy moments, was not always evident.

Augustine and the Fundamentalist's Daughter, 2011

In *Augustine and the Fundamentalist's Daughter* I reflected on how engagement with Augustine's writings over many years shaped me as a person and a scholar. I explored why certain features of Augustine's thought interested me while others—such as his doctrinal controversies—did not. In brief, I understood myself to be a "fundamentalist's daughter," damaged by a severe and demanding childhood religion, who found in *some* of Augustine's themes relief from the strictness of my childhood and youth. Augustine said: "I relaxed a little from myself."[4] "Getting over myself" became an important theme of my life.

I found in Augustine the groundbreaking (for me) suggestion that fear and "besetting sins" are not to be stamped out, "killed,"[5] but rather that the passion, the energy they carry is to be redeemed, "carried over" to fund love. Augustine wrote: "My weight is my love; by it I am carried wherever I am carried."[6] Could I *do* this? To recognize the value of this project is not to achieve it. It requires that I must *remember* and *relax into* the peculiar rhythm (systole and diastole) of struggle and acceptance Augustine described in his *Confessions*. Oh! What a strenuous and lifelong job it is to make a fearful person into a loving person, to say every day, "I will, with God's help."

---

4. *Cessavi de me paululum*; Augustine, *Confessions*, 7.14.
5. The language of many devotional manuals.
6. *Pondeus meus amor meum; eo feror quecumque feror*; Augustine, *Confessions*, 13.9.

Retirement Part II, 2011 to 2017

"On Getting Over Oneself," *Reading Ideologies*, 2011

An invitation to contribute an essay for a *feschscrift* in honor of Professor Mary Ann Talbot provided an opportunity to explore an interest I had since I wrote *Reading for Life* (discussed in chapter 5). Reading, frequently thought of as "abstract" by contrast with the concreteness of "experience," can, with attentiveness and reflection, offer "enlarged perspectives and suggest more generous attitudes towards oneself and others." Reading for life is "reading to try on new ways of thinking, feeling, and acting."

In North American society, attitudes of *suspicion* are necessary if we are not to become the helpless victims of ubiquitous frauds.[7] Suspicion is based on fear, and fear is reinforced by a public culture that constantly produces and circulates fear factors. Individuals who live in fear are likely to buy commodities to pacify and reassure themselves. In twenty-first-century American society, it is not unrealistic to fear unsolicited incursions on our finances and ideas.

Nevertheless, while we routinely practice suspicion in public life, we need to be able to *imagine*, to *picture*, what it might look and *feel like* to respond lovingly in personal life. Fiction, I claimed, can help us imagine loving relationships so that we do not automatically—by default—translate the suspicion with which we must regard advertisers and politicians into our personal lives. Lacking guides and models of loving behavior it is difficult to identify alternatives to the mistrust we practice in public life. Reading for life is a method for imagining achieving—or failing to achieve—loving relationships.

Novels can provide attitude-changing, and therefore life-changing, suggestions. As philosopher Suzanne Langer discussed in her important book, *Philosophy in a New Key*, the arts we live with educate—or fail to educate—our emotions. Historian Lynn Hunt persuasively documented the "real effects" eighteenth-century epistolary novels had on both private and public life. Eighteenth-century epistolary novels enabled a newly literate public to empathize with fictional characters unknown to them in life (especially the poor). Ability imaginatively to *feel* others' physical and emotional pain created altered attitudes, attitudes that led to the reform of punishment practices across Europe.[8]

---

7. After I had been the victim of a fraud involving several hundred dollars, a friend urged me to be more suspicious. I complained, "I don't want to live that way." She responded, "Well then, you can't have a telephone or a computer; you can't even get mail!"

8. In *Eichmann in Jerusalem*, Hannah Arendt described Eichmann's crime as

To illustrate, I considered four novelistic accounts of individuals who practiced profoundly counter-cultural behavior in personal situations of stress and grief. I discussed Ian McEwan's *Atonement*, Susan Howatch's *The Heartbreaker*, Sue Miller's *The Senator's Wife*, and Virginia Woolf's *Mrs. Dalloway*.

Getting Here from There: Conversations on Life and Work, with Hiroko Sakomura, 2011

This book began with my essay for the exhibition catalog, *The Vision and Art of Shinjo Ito* (discussed in chapter 6).[9] I was invited to give a lecture based on my essay at the North American venues of the exhibition—New York, Chicago, and Los Angeles. Every morning at breakfast in a hotel, the exhibition curator, Hiroko Sakomura, and I talked. We rapidly discovered that both of us as young women expected to marry, have children, and to have no further need to plan our lives. Through many struggles we both succeeded in achieving rich and pleasurable lives. We managed to have *both* children *and* demanding careers. Hiroko became a well-known and sought-after cultural producer, with a large staff and, at any one time, exhibitions in several cities across the world. I had become an author and tenured faculty member at Harvard University. The success of the North American exhibitions led to an invitation to give my lecture at the Tokyo home of Shinnyo-en Buddhism. After the lecture, Hiroko took me to her birthplace, Yamaguchi, in the beautiful mountains of northern Japan.

Getting Here from There began with our growing friendship and conversations in the North American exhibition cities. Except for the Introduction, the book consists entirely of these conversations. The title is a quotation from Harvard then-president Derek Bok. Amused that my teaching career began in California community colleges, he said jokingly, "You can't get here from there!"

Thinking that our conversations might interest and encourage others, we began to tape them. Hiroko's English was flawless; she had attended graduate school in the United States, so we were able to communicate with precision and depth about our experiences. Later, I transcribed and edited our tapes, and we began to consult publishers. We hoped to publish our

---

"thoughtlessness," which she defined as "inability to think from another's point of view."

9. "Seeing as Believing: Shinjo Ito and the Role of Vision in Religious Practice," in *The Vision and Art of Shinjo Ito*.

book simultaneously in English and Japanese; I would write the Introduction to the English edition, and Hiroko would introduce the Japanese edition. But the Japanese publisher Hiroko consulted told her, "If you two were famous, people would be interested in your lives." In short, although Hiroko thought that the book was especially needed in Japan, we had to be content with an English publisher.

Getting Here from There begins with thoughts about our childhood homes and the models we had for our personal choices as adults. We compared both the conditions that inhibited us and those that enabled us to achieve in our different societies. We talked about our habits, our relationships, and our styles of dressing. The middle section of the book is devoted to discussing the values that inform our professional and private lives. We conclude with features of our societies that concern us. We hope that our efforts were not entirely for our own aggrandizement but also for women and men of many races, ethnicities, and visions who will follow us. We think of ourselves as placeholders for others who will move into our places in our chosen professions.

"From Rape to Resurrection: Sin, Sexual Difference and Politics," *Augustine's* City of God: *A Critical Guide*, 2012

Augustine's mature work, *The City of God*, was written to persuade pagans that the so-called Sack of Rome was not caused by neglect of the Roman gods that had protected Rome for 800 years, and to reassure Christians that pagan accusations were inadmissible. But a more subtle and skillful argument permeates his text, namely, an original version of the history of the human race. From book 1, in which Augustine writes as an unlikely "rape crisis counselor," to the closing books of his epic in which Augustine insists, against scriptural suggestions and the belief of "many" that women will achieve the "perfect"—that is male—body in the resurrection, that female bodies will be retained in the resurrection. Female bodies, he writes, are not part of the punishment of the human race belonging to present existence, but are "natural" entities. In short, in *The City of God*, "female bodies became a paradigm of the experience of the human race, from rape to resurrection, from abjection to perfection." Female bodies, vulnerable to rape and unwanted childbearing, are Augustine's example of "used" bodies that, in the resurrection, "will be transformed to a body whose beauty is enjoyed "for itself alone." For Augustine, the female body is the paradigmatic human body, in its journey "from rape to resurrection."

I find several points of error or unclarity in the essay. For example, it was wrong to say that for Augustine "body and soul . . . seemed to him so distinguishable as to be separable." While it is true that Augustine considered it obvious that soul is greater and more valuable than body, his acknowledged fantasy of resurrected bodies in the last books of *The City of God* reveal his ability to imagine a "spiritual body" that is nevertheless a "real body," permeated throughout by spirit's "invulnerability, weightlessness, and incredible capacity for effortless movement and penetrating vision."

The passage is interlaced with the scriptural verse Augustine quoted more frequently than any other throughout his *oeuvre*, 1 Corinthians 13:12.[10] Augustine's inability to imagine a *present* practice that could begin to address the injustices of the earthly city in favor of the imagined justice and equality of the heavenly city rests on his dramatic syncrisis, now (*nunc*). . . then (*tunc*). His separation of present experience from resurrection experience permits him to evade "the [present] issue of power and its abuses." A telling verbal strategy enables this evasion. In the social dislocation brought about by the CE 410 Sack of Rome, he substitutes order (*ordo*) for power (*potestas*), ignoring the invisible power necessary to guarantee the social order. Augustine believed that (potentially) coercive power, "masked as natural and God-given order, [was] the only possible politics."

"Augustine and Freud: The Secularization of Self-Deception," *Augustine and Psychology*, 2012

Herbert Fingarette describes the dynamic of self-deception: I "take account of my situation and detect a condition which is relevant to my interests, but which would gravely disrupt my mental equilibrium if my attention were to focus on it. [So I] avoid turning my attention in that direction."[11] Self-deception, he writes, is "as ordinary and familiar a kind of mental activity as one can imagine"; it is woven into the deepest layers of habitual behavior.[12] "The falsification of memory—the adjustment, abbreviation, invention,

---

10. "We see now through a glass darkly, then, however, face to face."
11. Fingarette, *Self Deception*, 169.
12. Fingarette, *Self Deception*, 162.

even *omission* of experience—is common to us all, it is the business of psychic life."[13]

Both Augustine and Freud recognized the goal of human life to be the achievement of happiness. Yet both valued *unhappiness* as a necessary incentive for seeking happiness. A person will change fundamentally only if she is unhappy *enough*—and is willing to acknowledge her state. *Moderate* unhappiness can be smothered by the pleasures designated by one's society. In present-day North America these include consumerism and entertainment. Pleasures more-or-less effectively conceal endemic intimate unhappiness and indefinitely postpone or permanently preclude a search for a more satisfying condition. To conceal unhappiness, Freud wrote, "we cannot do without palliative remedies. . . . Something of this kind is indispensable."[14] Freud believed that as long as one is happy *enough*, or can, through self-deception, resist awareness of unhappiness, no cure is possible.

Are self-deceivers responsible for their own inability to change, or are they "helpless victims"? Hindus have long argued about whether grace is best described as the "cat-carrying method" or the "monkey-carrying method." In the cat-carrying method, the kitten collapses and its mother seizes it by the scruff of its neck while it dangles limply from the mother's mouth. The infant monkey, on the other hand, must climb onto the mother's back and hold on for dear life as she carries him. Augustine's prescription most closely resembles the cat-carrying method; he repeatedly, throughout his writings, pictures himself as utterly helpless and entirely dependent on God's forcible "turning his head" (*fovisti caput*).[15] Freud's prescription resembles the monkey-carrying method: the talking cure assumes that the patient must undertake the slow, committed work of analysis. Replacing Augustine's model in which one agent [God] does something *to* another agent [Augustine], Freud proposed that the talking cure is something two agents [analyst and analysand] do *together*.

Self-deception has a bad name. Augustine, Freud, and twentieth-century analyst Herbert Fingarette consider self-deception destructive. Its most immediate result is to preclude or inhibit the search for happiness. Indeed, if anything positive were found to be associated with it, this positive something would need to be renamed. However, in this article

13. McGrath, *Trauma*, 46.
14. Freud, *Civilization and Its Discontents*.
15. O'Connell, *Augustine's Early Theory*, 66.

I suggest that although the concept of self-deception has been useful to religious leaders, philosophers, and psychologists for centuries, the concept is imprecise, unwieldy and potentially dangerous.[16] The phrase itself connotes a negative judgment; it is reviewer-language, an accusation. Few people admit themselves to be guilty of self-deception, except perhaps in retrospect. The term covers too much murky ground. For example, the boundary between self-deception and optimism is faint and fungible; there are occasions and areas in which self-deception and optimism are impossible to distinguish. Freud's criteria for psychic health is relevant: ability to love and work characterizes psychic health; these abilities are strongly associated with optimism. "Self-deception" imbued with optimism need not mask unhappiness but can provide energy for work and love.

Do I deceive myself when I cautiously hope/expect that a loved one will recover from a terminal illness? Isn't my optimism *in the day there is more fruitful* than acceptance that he will die? It is still a beautiful world, I said to myself as my husband lay dying, accepting nonetheless that it was unlikely that a ninety-two-year-old would recover from a terminal illness. An admixture of acceptance and gratitude/optimism was needed. An onlooker might well name this attitude self-deception—or denial—another bullying word. But who has the unerring ability to identify what is "real"? Lacking that ability, we accept what is given with gratitude—and without enervating attempts to discern how nearly one's attitude matches the "reality" of the situation.

"The Resurrection of Body: Re-imagining Human Personhood in the Christian Tradition," *Theology, Aesthetics, and Culture: Responses to the Work of David Brown*, 2012

Theologian David Brown's insistence on the strong role of bodies and senses in Christian traditions requires a different model of "person" than is commonly understood. In this essay, after examining three understandings of "person," I reject the traditional model in which "person" is composed of stacked components, with body on the bottom and rational soul or mind on top. I also dismiss neuroscientists' model in which body produces and

---

16. The seventeenth-century English author Thomas Traherne said that the problem with misunderstanding a concept is that "What we misapprehend, we cannot use." *Centuries*, IV. 16.

enables mind. I accept Maxine Sheets-Johnstone's description of the "intelligent body," one entity, without "components." Neither "rational mind" nor controlling body can "believe" the Christian doctrine of bodily resurrection, I conclude, but an "intelligent body" *can*.

I suggest that belief in a bodily resurrection places new urgency on considering what it *means* to believe. If we think of belief as something done by the rational mind, the doctrine of the resurrection of body places an immense, if not intolerable, demand on twenty-first-century Christians. *But intelligent bodies believe in a different way than rational minds.* For intelligent bodies, to believe this doctrine is to commit to living *toward* it. In fact, to seek, *in the present,* to live out into the resurrection body, seems both a more realistic and a more demanding definition of belief than rational mind's assent.

I pointed out that Christians already *practice* the intelligent body, *behaving* as if we consider bodies and senses at the center of the "religion of the Word made flesh." Liturgies include *seeing* images that adorn our churches; we meet to sing (and thus to *breathe* together); we *touch* one another with a handshake, hug, or kiss, not merely in greeting or departing, but *liturgically,* as we say, "Peace be with you." We *hear* scriptures and sermons; we say together creeds and liturgical responses; we *taste* the Eucharistic elements. Indeed senses play a central role in Christian worship.

We *practice* the irreducible consanguinity of word and flesh. But we do not a*rticulate* the values that direct our sensory engagement. Rather, we *think* that Christianity is all about intellectual assent to creeds, beliefs, and scriptures. We value language very highly, so it is important to articulate, to *spell out* what we think we believe. What remains unarticulated tends to be ignored. There is self-contradiction in "silently thinking" that Christianity is all about language while "practicing" sensory engagement.[17]

This essay was my first foray into the more comprehensive account of the presence of the "intelligent body" (in the wings) throughout the history of Christianity that would later appear in *Beyond the Centaur.*

---

17. "The only criterion of Socratic thinking is . . . to be consistent with oneself." Arendt, *Thinking,* 186.

Recollections and Reconsiderations

The Wendell Cocktail: Depression, Addiction, and Beauty,
2012

My brother, Wendell, died in 2010, several months before his sixtieth birthday. Shortly before he suffered the series of strokes that killed him, Wendell sent me a large box full of lined notebooks containing his journals. He asked me to "release them as you think best." I thanked Wendell for them and replied that I would read them "when I can." It was several years before I found the leisure and energy to read them. Reeking of smoke, full of misspellings and incomplete sentences, and mottled with spilled liquids, they were *physically* difficult to read. They were also emotionally difficult.

Reading them, I asked myself whether Wendell's "dual diagnosis" problems were personal or social. They were demonstratively both, so I wrote about them as both. The social, characterized by lack of research and resources for patients who suffer from mental illness and the addiction with which they medicate, seemed intractable. Yet dual diagnosis patients constitute a huge social problem; approximately half of the people with mental illness medicate with an addiction. I hoped the book would have some effect on social consciousness and conscience on their behalf.[18] The personal—Wendell's personality and family, his bewildering mixture of anger and sensitivity to natural beauty, was easily demonstrated in his journals.

Wendell did not live to see my book, *The Wendell Cocktail*. I wonder whether he would have thought I got his situation (approximately) right. When I began to write, I assumed that mental illness is—or should be—curable. If sufficient resources were put into research, I thought, cures would be found. But what if this is not the case? What if the idea that mental suffering can be prevented or cured is illusory? What if mental illness cannot be "mastered"?

What if, rather than seeking cures for mental illness—"cures" that in the not-so-distant past have included horrifying abuses—we need to consider palliative care? Just as society has learned that dying people need not be tortured by attempted "cures," but rather need their suffering to be alleviated, it may be that people who suffer from mental illness can best be helped by palliative care. Millions of people who medicate with alcohol, marijuana, and various prescription and street drugs may be, in effect,

---

18. NAMI, National Association for Mental Illness, has recently recognized and offers some resources for dual diagnosis patients. See website.

trying to tell us this. Palliative care for the mentally ill is not a new idea; it is being practiced regularly, but further research could support and refine palliative care for the mentally ill. Drugs with greater efficiency and fewer dangers might be developed.

"Response" to *Augustine and the Fundamentalist's Daughter, Pastoral Psychology,* 2013

When authors send a book out into the world of readers we are lucky if we get one thoughtful review. Often we never know if anyone at all has read and thought about the book. The "Book Forum" of the journal, *Pastoral Psychology*, is a wonderful opportunity for reflections from different perspectives. I am very grateful for the four article-length reviews/responses to *Augustine and the Fundamentalist's Daughter* by Professors Donald Capps, Jennifer Hockenbery Dragseth, Kim Paffenroth, and Hugh Wire. I was invited to respond to these reviews in the same edition.

Several of the authors' comments clarified points in my book and prompted further thinking on my part. As Jennifer Hockenbery Dragseth points out, I am heavily formed and influenced by the Platonic tradition. Clearly, not the Platonism that identifies so strongly with rationality that its practitioner ought to be of pleasant disposition while being burned alive in the legendary bull of Phalaris, but rather the strain of Platonism represented by the Socratic insistence that the only requirement for thought is self-consistency. Sounds easy, but isn't.

How can we "self-consistently" live joyously, fulfilling "the chief end of man" (according to the Westminster Shorter Catechism), while the world we inhabit is filled with injustice, suffering, and danger? The contradiction cannot be rationally resolved, but the conundrum can—and must—be resolved by living fully in the present moment.[19] "It's the richness of the mixture," Saul Bellow's hero, Henderson the Rain King mutters. Neither the highs nor the lows in isolation from the other are overwhelming. Each frames the other; "it's the richness of the mixture."

---

19. An example: Christian Holy Week liturgies juxtapose the joyous triumph of Palm Sunday with the pain and apparent utter defeat of Good Friday. Palm Sunday (the parade, the acclamations) is usually experienced and interpreted as anticipating and heightening the overriding pain of Good Friday. But couldn't Palm Sunday be understood as establishing a foreshadowing or *link* to the joy of Easter?

Recollections and Reconsiderations

I am very grateful for these thoughtful reviews of *Augustine and the Fundamentalist's Daughter*.

"Art, Gender, and Religion," *The Cambridge Companion to Art and Religion*, 2014

Traditionally, artworks have been examined as moments in a history of style and/or in terms of their formal presentation. Considering the role of religion and gender in an artwork's communication entails exploring the artwork as a social and religious communication in its society of origin. An interdisciplinary approach examines the multiple and intimate *connections* within the fields of religion, gender, and art. Until recently, interdisciplinary work has been prevented by the prevalence of polemical protocols. Traditionally, a scholar's work is furthered by demolishing the work of another scholar, "making scholarly exchanges defensive and aggressive rather than responsive to, and building on the insights of scholars in other fields." If religion is to be understood "on location," however, interdisciplinary work is necessary, as religion is woven into the images, literature, social arrangements, and "silent thoughts" or assumptions of a community.

The study of women's activities in historical communities is not the same as the examination of gender socialization within communities. "The enormous amount of attention to women, their 'nature,' dress, and roles, reveals women's power and thus the importance, from the masculinist perspective, of controlling and subordinating that power." I conclude: "The future of gender, imagery, and religious imagination lies in integrating the feminist project of reclaiming women's agency and eliminating women's oppression with the religious studies agenda of critical understanding and appropriation of religious images."

I would now add a further impediment to fruitful interdisciplinary work from the side of Religious Studies. The early identification of Christianity with texts, beliefs, and philosophy, well established by the end of the fourth century, has effectively led to ignoring the importance of religious images in the formation of Christian sensibilities. Although the work of contemporary scholars is presently challenging this preoccupation with language, religious images are not yet taken as seriously as religious language in departments of theology and religious studies. Nevertheless, progress is occurring; when I began teaching history of Christianity at HDS using slides as primary texts, I carried my own projector to my classroom.

Now state-of-the-art visual equipment is built-in and the room can be darkened easily so that students do not need to strain to see the projected image whose vibrant hues are lost in a room with unscreened windows.

I note a further hindrance to the interdisciplinary exploration of religion, art, and gender from the side of women's studies. In seeking conversation among colleagues at a major university, I found that many colleagues in women's studies and gender studies in other departments of the university were strongly judgmental of religion, regarding it as an undifferentiated category. The "religion" they loved to hate had damaged, limited, and hurt them as children and young adults. Unresponsive to arguments about the enormous varieties of religion, they insisted on excluding from scholarship every "taint" of religion. In several cases the historical women they researched and endeavored to understand explicitly acknowledged the role of religion in authorizing their voices and activities. Yet contemporary scholars ignored and/or hastily transferred these acknowledgements to *political* agenda. I hesitate to give examples! For intellectual as well as personal reasons, many scholars have not recovered from negative assumptions about religion that originated in the enlightenment and the scientific revolution.

When these prejudices are overcome, what lively and colorful portraits of historical communities can be painted! The rewards of getting over field blinders are evident immediately.

Beyond the Centaur: Imagining the Intelligent Body, 2014

> The centaur was described in ancient literature and sculpture as perpetually struggling with its two natures; wild as an untamed horse, he was also a civilized human. In the centaur, barbarism and wisdom were constantly in violent conflict for ascendency.

A great deal depends on the story we tell ourselves about who we are. For many centuries the centaur has been our favorite story about the nature(s) of humans: That story is that humans are hastily assembled antagonistic components of unequal value. Maxine Sheets-Johnstone's description of the "intelligent" or "first-person" body tells a different story.[20]

Part I of *Beyond the Centaur* explores historical conceptions of bodies, from stacked components to the intelligent body. Part II considers how we

---

20. See chapter 2 for Sheets-Johnstone's description of the "intelligent body."

might experience our lives differently if we thought of ourselves as intelligent bodies rather than as hierarchically stacked components. Chapters discuss how, in distinction from *assembled parts*, intelligent bodies move, feel, think, believe, and die. The book seeks to document that the intelligent body has often been assumed throughout the history of Christianity, but has not been spelled out. Body, in Thomas Traherne's observation, has been "misapprehended," and the problem with misapprehension in that "what we misapprehend, we cannot use."[21]

The Long Goodbye: Dementia Diaries, 2017

Like *The Wendell Cocktail*, writing this book was grief work. But I also thought it important to give a more balanced account of the experience of loving a dementia patient than the horror stories currently circulating in popular literature. Certainly, the horror stories were there, but my experience was not all horror stories. There were also opportunities to learn, especially to "get over myself," and there were moments of great beauty. If one expects only horror stories, one will *notice* nothing but horror stories. If they are not *looked for*, other experiences will be overlooked or ignored; they often go by rapidly. But if one looks for learning experiences and moments of beauty, they will occur. I wrote the book to prompt those who love someone with dementia to notice opportunities to learn and poignant moments of beauty.

My *method*, illustrated and advocated in *The Long Goodbye*, can be called the "Beowulf method."[22] Beowulf's trusty sword, well-documented veteran of many successful conquests, simply melted (a male nightmare) when the hero faced the monster. Desperately seeking a usable weapon he notices a sword hanging on the wall. He grabs it and with it slays the monster. The moral of the story is this: when recommended methods fail, rather than surrender in despair, one must look around and seek alternatives *in the vicinity*. The story taught me that, although few of the "tried and true" methods of relationship *work* when loving someone with dementia, there are, *within the situation*, creative possibilities that *do* work.

The Long Goodbye describes my husband's decade-long struggle with dementia and my efforts to love him during the bewildering years when he was still at home, and the last three years when he was in an assisted living

---

21. Traherne, *Centuries of Meditation*, 4.16.
22. From the Norse saga, *Beowulf*.

residence. The book offers no conclusions about the "best way" or the "right way" to relate to a dementia patient, but *suggests* approaches that helped *me* and might help someone else in a similar situation.

Once again I asked myself, Is this a personal or a social problem? A little research showed that it is adamantly both. Dementia presents loved ones and caregivers with both logistical and philosophical dilemmas. I sought to do everything I possibly could to brighten my husband's days; I also wanted to treat him in a way that would not eventuate in later feelings of guilt and regret. But forgiving myself when I was unable to help Owen due to exhaustion was also important. Now, two years after his death, I am content to acknowledge *both* that "I did the best I could," *and* that it wasn't enough, could not possibly have been enough.

In chapter 8 I consider my prototype and inspiration for the project of critically recalling and reviewing my publications, Augustine's *Retractationes,* volume two of his autobiography.

PART IV

Chapter 8

Reading Augustine Reading Augustine

cessavi de me paululum"
CONFESSIONS 7.14

respire in te paululum
CONFESSIONS 13.14

I.

THINKING THROUGH HIS PUBLISHED works in old age, Augustine sometimes confessed to impatience and something that sounds to me—having had a similar experience while rereading my publications—like boredom. His critical review of his publications was poignantly human; he was "loath to admit that he was ever distinctly wrong on a point of substance."[1] Nevertheless, he corrected his writings from the perspective of hindsight, ending the project in CE 427 without completing it:[2]

---

1. O'Donnell, *Augustine*, 301.
2. Chapter 1 describes further the circumstances in which he wrote the *Retractationes*.

- he admitted forgetfulness of what he meant when writing a particular treatise;[3]
- he remarked regarding *On the Immortality of the Soul*: "It is . . . so obscure on account of its complicated reasoning and its brevity that, when I read it, it taxes even my own attention and I myself can barely understand it";[4]
- he admitted, "I have been unable to remember what I meant when I said . . .";
- he confessed, "all of this was said very rashly";[5]
- he acknowledged that his book on lying is "obscure, complicated, and altogether difficult to understand";[6]
- he corrected words that were misleading, or not exactly what he hoped to convey;[7]
- he noticed that his early writings demonstrate an incomplete conversion from philosophical to ecclesiastical language;[8]
- he questioned the optimism of his early writings;
- he recognized that his lack of clarity sometimes resulted in misunderstandings;
- he rectified a misquotation from scripture ("All order is from God," Romans 13:1);[9]
- he acknowledged a significant change of mind, refuting his former statement, made in *Against the Party of Donatus*, in which he said, "I am displeased that schismatics are violently coerced to communion by the force of a secular power." He made this statement he said,

---

3. Augustine, *Retractationes*, 1.5.3.
4. Augustine, *Retractationes*, 1.5.1
5. Augustine, *Retractationes*, 1.5.3.
6. Augustine, *Retractationes*, 1.2.6.
7. Augustine, *Retractationes*, 1.6.2
8. Augustine, *Retractationes*, 1.3.2.
9. Augustine, *Retractationes*, 1.12.8. The quotation should read: "The things that exist have been ordained by God." Augustine often quoted scripture from memory. I have found that it is always worth looking up his scriptural quotations. Frequently his *memory* of a verse very slightly supports the argument in which he quotes it! Here, Augustine's strong predilection for social order (understandable, in the chaos of the early fifth century) slightly adjusts the verse he (thinks he) remembers.

"because I had not yet learned either how much their impunity would dare, or to what extent the application of discipline could bring about their improvement";[10]

- he wrote, commenting on his book *On the Divination of Demons*: "I spoke on a very obscure subject with a more daring asseveration than I should."[11]

2

The only work Augustine remembered with uncomplicated pleasure as he wrote his *Retractationes* was his *Confessions*.

> The thirteen books of my confessions praise the just and good God for *both the bad and the good that I did*, and they draw a person's mind and emotions toward him. As for myself, that is how they affected me when they were being written, and that is how they affect me when they are being read. What others may think of them is up to them, but I know that they have pleased and do please many of the brothers a great deal.[12]

Confessions is one of Augustine's few nonpolemical published works; nor was he entertaining others' questions. Though he addressed his musings to God, his human audience—brothers in Christ, lay and clerical—was firmly in mind as he wrote; he feared laughter at his intimate revelations. But his project and primary attention was on collecting and retracing God's leading through "the bad and the good that I did." And that is what he noticed when he reread his confessions. Augustine's goal was not to correct doctrinal error—though the *Confessions* contain honest accounts of his struggle to understand central doctrines such as the incarnation of Jesus Christ. Rather he sought to collect his life as one entity, to re-member the people, events, and personal struggles that together constitute his life as God's leading, not as a concatenation of one thing after another. When he reread his confessions—as when he wrote them—his attention was not on the damages to himself and others that resulted from his youthful choices, but on the shaping hand of God in his life.[13] God's leading is the thread that wove together the colorful strands of his life.

10. Augustine, *Retractationes*, 2.31.
11. Augustine, *Retractationes*, 2.56.
12 Augustine, *Retractationes*, 2.6; emphasis added.
13. Augustine's apparent indifference to damages to others— such as the fate of the

Augustine deplored his youthful hedonism, blindness and stubbornness. He was judgmental rather than critical, condemning rather than understanding. Nevertheless, he saw in retrospect that— through no merit of his own—he had *learned* from his bad as well as from his good behavior. On the one hand, he affirmed the life to which *all* his struggles had led him, but he was also ambivalent about the *path* by which he arrived there, even as he understood that God's leading had intimately informed his flailing efforts. At this point, he fails the Socratic self-consistency test!

Augustine's zeal to defend what he considered right Christian belief and doctrine led him frequently to use harsh language. Although he did not urge his own life choice of monastic celibacy on anyone else, he was intolerant of a fellow Christian theologian and monk, Jovinian, who argued that Christian marriage is as worthy a condition in which to live a Christian life as vowed virginity. In his old age, even though long since distanced from the heat of controversy, he called Jovinian "a monster" and a heretic.[14] He was more accepting about alternative scriptural interpretations than he was about alternatives to his personal choices. Thirty years before, referring to a Hebrew Bible passage, Augustine had written:

> Can you not see how foolish it is out of all that abundance *of perfectly true meanings which can be extracted from those* words rashly to assert that one particular meaning was the one that Moses had chiefly in mind, and thereby in one's pernicious quarrelsomeness to offend charity herself?[15]

No such generosity characterized his response to Jovinian's suggestion that the Christian life could be lived as faithfully in marriage as in celibacy.

Augustine's most characteristic doctrines reveal his need to protect himself from recognizing that God might have other characteristics than love. "When Augustine makes his most cherished assertions about his god (sic), we need to hear that at the same time he is giving tacit voice to his deepest anxieties."[16] Indeed, his "most original and nearly single-handed creation,"[17] the doctrine of original sin, can be understood as functioning to release Augustine from the necessity of understanding God as a tyrant who

---

women with whom he was intimate and the friends he introduced to Manichaeism—often irritate his readers.

14. Augustine, *Retractationes*, 2.48. 1.
15. Augustine, *Confessions*, 12.25.
16. O'Donnell, *Augustine*, 293.
17. O'Donnell, *Augustine*, 296.

judges and damns without mercy or attention to individual struggles. If *all* humans are worthy of damnation, God's great mercy in rescuing an elect few can become our focus.

Furthermore, Augustine's doctrine of predestination stops short of acknowledging that God predestines the *massa damnata*. Centuries later Luther and Calvin saw that the *foreknowledge* of an omniscient and omnipotent being necessarily constitutes foreordination. Augustine would not go there; against logic, he insisted that God only had *foreknowledge* of the damned and the elect. These efforts to maintain God's love as his essential characteristic at the cost of incoherence (original sin) and logic (predestination) reveal Augustine's intransigent commitment to God-is-love. In a homily on 1 John 4:16, Augustine quoted the verse, "God is love," commenting, "and that is all you need to know about God."[18]

3

Teaching an author of whom many people have differing, if not directly opposite, opinions, I attempted to move those who disliked Augustine to what I thought of as a "deeper understanding." Students often began study of Augustine with settled opinions I considered shallow, prejudices based on secondary authors and tendentious translations. A student once complained that I would not allow students to criticize Augustine until they loved him. I acknowledge some truth in that! I wanted them to see him as a flawed, suffering and struggling human being like ourselves—neither the angel nor the devil he was often held to be. Like all of us, he was, to some extent, the victim of inherited assumptions and inadequate language. *Tout comprendre c'est tout pardoner*, I thought.

I have only recently realized that Augustine's ideas, as interpreted by his friends through the centuries, have *both* benefitted *and damaged* human well-being. Because I studied and taught Augustine in an environment in which he was an object of cultural scorn, I attempted to tip that consensus in the direction of recognizing his energy, passion, and—oh yes—his beautiful Latin. Had I taught in a culture that revered him as the master, the authority and unquestioned spokesperson for Christianity, I would have been more eager to question his assumptions, worldview, and interpretations of doctrine. Instead I chose not to notice the damages, either evident in his writings, or as later authors interpreted him. I thought that *some*

18. *Homilies on the First Epistle of John*, seventh homily.

of Augustine's ideas and passions could—and should—be rehabilitated. I declined to undermine the relentless energy with which he advocated participation in God's love by acknowledging his sexism, his animus toward opponents, and his use of power. I sought to understand Augustine as a person, before God, who did the best he could—and it wasn't good enough. It is all that human beings can do.

4

Stephan Greenblatt has recently discussed Augustine's "invention of sex."[19] Clearly, his title is a misnomer. Augustine did not invent sex, but he did identify sex as evidence and proof of "original sin," a concept that preceded Augustine and even Christianity by millennia.[20]

Original sin names a presentiment in Judaism and Christianity that something is not quite *right* about humanity, and is evident in every human being. The third-century Christian, Tertullian, had called this undertow of human life "weakness" (*vitium*). Augustine's youthful experience suggested a much darker, more pervasive and profound taint that he named "sin" (*peccatum*). It was he who soldered original sin to sex, a conceptual move both brilliant and fatal—brilliant, because it made what had been a vague nagging feeling of inadequacy into a powerful and well-nigh universal *experience*; fatal, because it "spoiled the fun" (Greenblatt's phrase), for generations of Christians who inherited the institutional and practical effects of Augustine's authority. In Augustine's vivid Latin, an abstract idea became performative, *experiential*. It is, however, not the only teaching for which Augustine should be remembered.

---

19. Greenblatt, "Invention of Sex," 24–28.
20. Williams, *Original Sin, passim*.

Chapter 9

Recollections and Reconsiderations

> Words, words, as if all worlds were there.
> ROBERT CREELEY

1

I HAVE STUDIED THE history of the Christian movement with attentiveness and passion for over fifty years. Alongside, and tightly woven into the great beauty of Christian liturgy, literature, music, and images are strategies by which Christians have fought against and excluded difference. Usually, "critical historians" expose the cruelties, blindness, and intransigence of Christians in the dominantly Christian West, while "church historians" gloze over these in order to revel in the *beauty* of the Christian movements. However, a responsible historian must see the beauty and the abuses *simultaneously*. One cannot be collapsed into the other; both must be recognized and acknowledged.

The French philosopher Michel Foucault described two different kinds of power. He named the power to attract *strong* power. While the power to attract is *working*, while it is able to entice most members of a society to behave in ways that reinforce authority, there is no need to invoke "weak power," coercion. However, weak power, though it may not be onstage, is always in the wings, to be called upon when "strong power" loses its attraction. The two kinds of power *work together* at all times; they must be understood as two sides of the same coin rather than as separate strategies. Like drawings in which either a duck or a rabbit pops into the eye, it is exceedingly difficult to see both at once. Like Augustine, most people *see* and value *either* order or power, not the duck and the rabbit simultaneously.

In what follows I reflect on the assumptions that lie beneath and support the abuses that have haunted Christianity. I do not consider the evident abuses—the persecution and murder of witches and heretics, wars fought against "infidels," or the everyday injustices of Christian institutions and societies. These are on record. Instead I consider the "silent thoughts" or assumptions by which harms were committed and rationalized. It is, I believe, the duty of a loving eye to notice and acknowledge abuses. It is in the spirit of love for the Christian traditions, then, that I say what I see to be Christian history's endemic problems.

Language

Some influential early Christians, like Justin Martyr, seeking a cultural niche for Christianity, described Christianity as an alternative to classical philosophy. In order to gain credence with philosophies in which body was to be "overlooked"—literally "looked over," the central role of bodies has been ignored or disparaged in the practice of Christianity, while soul/mind was assiduously cultivated. Thus, massive attention has been paid to precision in doctrine and creedal *language*. From earliest Christianity, and becoming explicit in fourth-century ecumenical councils, there was tacit agreement that the words defining Christian belief are essential. Christians have been willing to break communion with other Christians, to fight, kill, and be killed for creedal and theological words. Many twenty-first century Christians, inheritors of that ancient assumption about the essence of Christianity, continue to think that Christian belief consists of cognitive assent to the particular language in doctrines and creeds.

It is startling to me that there has never been a conflict over language-use similar to the conflict in Eastern Orthodoxy over image-use. In the iconoclastic controversy, iconoclasts charged that the hoi polloi were worshipping, not its prototype but the image itself (idolatry). In the controversy, thousands of monks, the defenders of icons (inconophiles), were slaughtered. The careful definitions of the Second Council of Nicaea (CE

787) ended the first wave of controversy, but a second wave erupted until a council affirmed the definitions of 787, and image use was restored in 843.[1] Similar blood baths have occurred in the West over words, yet there have been no controversies over *word idolatry*. Does language represent sacred reality with any greater precision, intimacy, and transparency than images? I think not, but the language of creeds and beliefs has been taken with the utmost seriousness *as if it were itself* the reality for which it stands. This is idolatry.

Language idolatry has been at the root of conflicts among Christians throughout history. Words, especially the highly condensed and freighted language of creeds, *invite* a variety of interpretations and thus debates, quarrels, and wars. Creeds, *necessarily* stated in language, *always* carry the possibility, nay the inevitability, of multiple interpretations. Scriptural language is also vulnerable to alternative interpretations—on a continuum from literal to figurative. Yet each increment of doctrinal precision has resulted in large groups of Christians who suddenly realize that the language approved by a council does not accurately define the reality to which/whom they pray.

When language is valued as a transparent expression of Christian truth, arguments are inescapable.[2] Throughout the medieval centuries, dissidents were executed for alternative interpretations. The most violent conflicts, articulated in religious language, but also composed of social, institutional, and liturgical loyalties, occurred in the sixteenth century reformations. These conflicts over beliefs and practices evolved into the Thirty Years War of the seventeenth century, 1618–1648.[3]

The most effective way to dispute an assumption is not to attack it frontally, however. Pointing out its dangers and inadequacies—much less going to war over it—is less effective than proposing a more fruitful and promising understanding. In a time when doctrinal differences were

---

1. Iconoclasts charged that people worshipped images who were unable to distinguish between the kind of veneration appropriate to images of saints and angels (*dulia*), divine figures (*hyperdulia*) and God (*latria*).

2. In 1054 Greek Orthodoxy split from Western Christianity over the use of one word: *filioque*. The issue was the Western addition of *filioque* (and the Son) to the creed, specifying that the Holy Spirit proceeds from the Father *and* the Son, challenging the Orthodox preference for thinking of the procession of the Holy Spirit from the Father *through* the Son.

3. Scholars estimate that up to three-fifths of Germany's 16 million inhabitants were killed in the Thirty Years War.

tearing nations apart and destroying millions of lives, the English theologian Richard Hooker advocated the central importance of *participation* in worship and the sacraments, minimizing the importance of defining precisely what occurs in that participation. Rejecting assent to a creed as a criterion of membership, he said that the only question that should be asked of a potential member is: Will you worship with us using the *Book of Common Prayer*?

Another kind of problem with language occurs in the Western contemporary post-Christian public sphere. Christians often claim *knowledge* of beliefs that can only be matters of faith. Because they experience inner conviction they say, for example, "I know that there is a life after death." But according to the commonly accepted public criterion for claiming knowledge, the so-called "scientific method," Christians don't—and can't—*know*; Christians *believe*. Words are defined by public understanding; a word cannot be given a private meaning *and expect to be understood* in the secular marketplace. The right word for personal knowledge that cannot be established by the scientific method is *belief*. But in common parlance "belief" has been compromised; it presently carries a tentative tone. Yet "I believe" carries the robust weight of my experiential "knowledge."

Soul

So much depends upon the story we tell ourselves about ourselves, both as individuals and as human beings. A book would be needed to trace the meanings of "soul" in Judaism and Greek philosophy. In Plato's *Apology*, Socrates defined soul as an entity that abandons the biodegradable body at death and lives on immortally. Immortality defines the high value of "the soul," thought of as separate and separable from body, a reified entity or component, housing both rationality and spirituality.

Although it is not a Christian belief, this understanding of soul has enjoyed a long half-life in Christianity. Belief in the immortality of the soul has undermined Christians' commitment to the integrity of person as articulated in fundamental Christian doctrines. It has caused not only confusion, but a distinctly non-Christian organization of values by which bodies of all kinds—human, animal, and the earth's body—have been ignored at best, and violated at worst.

Identification of soul as the function or activity of the intelligent body that listens and speaks to God is ubiquitous in the history of the Christian traditions. But it should be understood and acknowledged that soul is not a separate or separable entity, but a way Christians try to describe a feature of the intelligent body, the body of creation, of Jesus's Incarnation, and the "real body," as Augustine insisted, of the promised resurrection.

Dichotomies

The perennial Western predilection for dichotomizing and hierarchicalizing has governed the values endemic to Christianity: soul and body; man and woman; Christ, the head, and the Church figured as the Body of Christ. In the history of Western thought, this logic has created multiple oppositions structuring philosophy and theology: subject/object, mind/body, nature/culture. Implicit in these dichotomies is the dichotomy good/bad, pure/impure. The first side of the dichotomy is elevated over the second because it designates the unified, the self-identical, whereas the second side lies outside the unified as the chaotic, formless that always threatens to break the unity of the good.[4] On the practical level, gender assumptions, expectations, and arrangements in Christian societies depend on the dichotomy male and female. In *Carnal Knowing*, I examined the multiple injustices, masquerading as "just the way it is," based on this dichotomy.

Appeals to Unity

Throughout the history of Christianity a heavy toll in human pain accompanied calls to unity, conceptualized as unanimity. Plotinus's image of unity as a choir singing harmoniously is a more useful and flexible metaphor. "Harmony" allows each person to sing their own note; it also implies enjoyment of the sound created by a choir of voices singing different notes.

Repetitious calls for unity throughout the history of Christianity strongly indicate both the continuous diversity of Christian belief and practice and an endemic fear of diversity. Across the Christian centuries, different criteria of what constitutes unity have been proposed. In the mid-third century, Cyprian, bishop of Carthage insisted that the bishop's beliefs and practices are normative and authoritative. Obedience to the bishop, he said, *is* the criterion of unity. In *On the Unity of the Church*, he argued against a time-honored North African value, namely, leadership by the Holy Spirit.

---

4. Young, *Justice*, 99.

The Holy Spirit's leadership threatened the bishop's authority; it was unpredictable and undisciplined; it might appear in anyone at any time. In fact, Montanist Christians, advocates for the Spirit's leadership, appointed women preachers and prophets. By contrast, Cyprian's authority was partly based on his ability to control consecrated virgins. He claimed that a bishop holds the absolute authority of a *paterfamilias* over virgins' dress and behavior. He also claimed authority over confessors—Christians condemned and awaiting execution for their belief. Based on their proven willingness to die for Christian belief, Carthaginian confessors had assumed authority to forgive sins, a power, Cyprian said, that belongs solely to the bishop. More than a little self-interest can be detected in Cyprian's struggle to maintain and implement bishops' authority.

In the fourth century a different interpretation of unity emerged. Ecumenical councils defined Christian unity as intellectual assent to a creed—that is, to the particular *wording* of the creed as approved by ecumenical councils. This definition of unity continued to dominate for many centuries. But, as I have noted, creeds, which sought to focus and clarify Christian doctrine, also created divisions. In the fifth century, large numbers of Christians, representing huge geographical areas, disagreed and split from Nicaean Christianity. Until churches achieved sufficient power to coerce others, this was not necessarily a negative development. However, by the end of the fourth century, the assumption that creedal unity is the centerpiece and defining characteristic of Christianity led to the first executions of dissident Christians.[5]

Although a single historical moment cannot be named as the moment when creedal belief was definitively challenged as the *sine qua non* of Christian faith, the Wars of Religion culminating in the 1648 Peace of Westphalia, marks a general fatigue in Western Europe with religious carnage based on adherence to a creed.[6]

2

Contemporary political philosopher Iris Marion Young has analyzed besetting problems with appeals to "unity" and "community." Such appeals, she says, mask a "logic of identity" by which members are expected to conform

---

5. Priscillian (in 386 CE) and Priscillianists; see O'Donnell, *Augustine*, 267.

6. In a whimsical moment I imagine God pondering the theological and doctrinal controversies of the Christian centuries, shaking his head and saying, "It doesn't matter."

to similar—if not identical—religious, political, and social values.[7] She finds such appeals coercive; they deny and exclude difference, converting the "merely different" into the "absolutely other."

Young proposes a different model: the city, vivid, energetic, and rich with diversity of all kinds. She defines city life as "the being together of strangers . . . clusters of people with affinities—families, social group networks, voluntary associations, neighborhood networks—a vast array of small 'communities.'" The city is a place where strangers meet and interact in the public arena of "politics, commerce and festival."[8] She proposes that the city supplies a more inclusive model than does community for accommodating difference. In the city, the goal cannot be rational transcendence of difference. Difference, she suggests, is precisely the factor that supplies color, interest, and excitement to human interactions.

Augustine made a similar suggestion—with one important difference. His disillusionment with life in the world of the later Roman Empire prompted him to make the huge leap of placing the "city of God" in another world, the heavenly world of the resurrection of body. He recommended that Christians practice *now* the fundamental characteristic of the city of God, namely love.

How inclusive can Christians be without losing the "thread"? Is there an alternative to unity defined as obedience to the bishop (Cyprian) or as cognitive assent to legislated creeds? Can another "thread" be identified? Could it be, as Richard Hooker suggested, a common *practice* rather than an infallible leader or a verbal formula? In isolation, neither the fictitious stand-alone body, nor the equally fictitious immortal soul can commit to the religion of the Word made flesh. Intelligent bodies are the only entity able to commit to the religion of the Incarnation. Could the essential unity, then, be intelligent bodies gathered together with a common commitment to becoming loving people, followers of the perfectly loving Jesus Christ, in the particular circumstances of our individual and communal lives?

As Augustine taught in his homilies on 1 John, God is love, and love is not (or is not primarily) a feeling, but a *practice*. Love is physical, a participation that is both symbolized and actualized in sharing the Eucharistic celebration: "This is my body, given for you." The Fourth Lateran Council (CE 1215) declared the Eucharistic *elements* to be the "body of Christ": "To carry out the *mystery of unity*, we ourselves receive from him the body that

---

7. Young, *Justice*, 98.
8. Young, *Justice*, 237.

he himself received from us."⁹ But I suggest that it is not the bread and the wine themselves, but the *activity of assembling and sharing the Eucharistic feast* that is the thread, the essential core and practice of Christian faith. According to the gospels, Christ said, "Do *this* in memory of me."¹⁰

Distracted from a history of diversity by persistent admonitions to unity, we imagine that the traditional picture of "unity" disturbed by "heresy" accurately represents the steady development of orthodoxy over alternative interpretations of scripture and beliefs in the history of Christian movements. But this picture is inaccurate, a self-serving fantasy. Moreover, it is not the history that Christians need to meet present challenges. The twenty-first century in the West is one of increasing inclusiveness, as churches ordain women and gay and lesbian Christians, and as Christians establish relations of mutual interest and learning with people of other religions. Rather than a history that claims unity by repetitiously and violently rejecting diversity, present Christians need to understand ourselves as living in one historical moment in a very long history of diversity.

Conversion

Christian history offers numerous examples of conversion experiences. Probably the most influential of these is Augustine's conversion, narrated in book 8 of his *Confessions*. The experience, described by Augustine and reiterated by Martin Luther, John Bunyan, and many others, is of a dramatic event, preceded by years of desperate seeking.¹¹ William James's *Varieties of Religious Experience* (1902) identifies two fundamentally different religious experiences, the "once-born," and the "twice-born."¹² James's analysis of twice-born Christians acknowledges that although it is the dramatic moment of conversion that captures attention, it most often, as in Augustine's experience, results from a long process of seeking, of "coming

---

9. Emphasis added.

10. Eating together defines the most primitive communal act of animate beings; Valantasis, *Dazzling Bodies*, 3.

11. The intelligent body, always waiting in the wings, storms onstage in Augustine's account of his conversion, a physical event replete with emotional torment, tears, and thrashing body.

12. James adopts Francis W. Newman's designations and description of "once-born" and twice-born;. *Varieties*, 68.

to understand," and of multiple experiences. In their descriptions, both Augustine and Luther foreshorten their accounts of conversion for dramatic effect.

Once-born religious experience lacks drama and thus has not had the same attention as the twice-born, who enjoy also the "credit of the proposer(s)";[13] as authoritative Christians like Augustine and Luther implicitly present their own experience as normative. Thus, once-born Christians frequently feel inferior to those who have experienced a sensational conversion. In fact, the twice-born experience is considered normative in some religious environments—from the revivalism of Pietism in eighteenth-century England and America, to the Billy Graham campaigns of mid-twentieth-century North America. Growing up in a revivalist church and home, as a child I was often unable to sleep at night, fearing that I had not had the mandatory religious experience, so that if I were to die in the night, I would go to hell.

A once-born Christian, James writes, is likely to "see God, not as a strict Judge, not as a Glorious Potentate, but as the animating Spirit of a beautiful harmonious world, Beneficent and Kind, Merciful as well as Pure."[14] He quotes:

> A child who is early taught that he is God's child, that he may live and move and have his being in God, and that he has, therefore, infinite strength in hand for the conquering of any difficulty, will take life more easily, and probably will make more of it, than one who is told that he is born the child of wrath and wholly incapable of good.[15]

Indeed, one who has been taught that she is "a child of wrath and wholly incapable of good," is all too familiar with the deleterious effects of such teaching. I can only look with envy at the once-born child of happy temperament, gratitude for life, and calm sleep.

---

13. John Locke recommended that truths of revelation should be accepted "on the credit of the proposer;" *Essay Concerning Human Understanding*, quoted in Miles, *Word Made Flesh*, 374.
14. James, *Varieties*, 68.
15. James, *Varieties*, 70.

Recollections and Reconsiderations
Images of God's Love for Humanity

The assumption that sacrifice is the strongest proof of love has had a long history of influence in the history of Judaism and Christianity. Two images, one from the Hebrew Bible, one from the New Testament, articulate and stabilize this conviction. First, in the story of Abraham and Isaac, God tells Abraham that to prove his commitment to God he must kill his beloved only son, Isaac. Abraham is about to carry out this order, but is stopped as he raises the knife to strike his son by the provision of an alternative sacrifice. The paradigm asks the believer, what/who do you love most? Then the believer is asked to sacrifice the most-loved object as proof of commitment to God. In the New Testament the paradigm is repeated and fulfilled in the (verbal and visual) image of the crucifixion of God's beloved only son. Throughout Christian history the paradigm has been reinterpreted. Because God sacrificed his own beloved son for the salvation of humanity which he "so loved," humans are not asked to prove love for God by killing a beloved child. Instead, sexuality, a person's most intimate and pleasurable gift, has been identified as the human good that must be sacrificed, replaced by vowed celibacy, for Christian "overachievers."[16]

As discussed in my 2008 book, *A Complex Delight*, crucifixion images became numerous and popular in Western Europe in an historical moment in which societies were rapidly changing from medieval home-based commerce to professional—read "patriarchal"—guilds to which women were not admitted. Because of guilds, "women lost social, economic, and legal power."[17]

I called attention to an image of God's love for humanity, popular in late medieval and early modern liturgical paintings and sculpture: the Virgin with one breast exposed, usually offering nourishment to the infant Christ.[18] The theology supporting the image of the Virgin with an exposed breast, and the theology underlying the crucifixion scene reveal different interpretations of how love is shown. The crucifixion image represents God's love for humanity as fully demonstrated in the sacrificial death of his only Son for the salvation of the world, tacitly suggesting that love is best demonstrated by sacrifice. The image of the Virgin offering her breast to the

---

16. Robin Lane Fox's term, *Pagan and Christian*. Another interpretation of celibacy is that it is a *sexual* choice, not a sacrifice of sexuality. But the popular interpretation, circulated in devotional manuals, was sacrifice.

17. Miles, *Complex Delight*, 79.

18. See above, 137ff., for further discussion of the Virgin's exposed breast.

infant Christ presents the provision of life, nourishment, and loving care as the strongest demonstration of love.

In the third century CE, Clement of Alexandria described God as Mother, an image that recurs in several Christian authors, such as the fourteenth-century recluse, Julian of Norwich. *Both images, as well as others that have been—or might be—proposed, are needed* to characterize and communicate so great a mystery. Each image communicates an important aspect of God's love; no single image can communicate its full range. Both images are scriptural or implied in scripture. Both the crucifixion scene and the Virgin's nourishing breast are gender specific, referencing either a father's or a mother's love. Both are needed. I repeat: *no one image* is adequate to express the greatest proclamation of Christian theology, namely that God loves and cares for humanity. Multiple images are needed to make this immense and mysterious assertion accessible.

Other images picturing God's love for humanity have been popular. During the times of persecution, Christian catacombs held multiple images of God's care and deliverance: Daniel in the lion's den, Jonah and the great fish, banquet scenes, and Christ the Good Shepherd, to name only a few. After the Peace of the Church, images of paradise proliferated on apses of the new lavish cathedrals across the Roman world.[19]

Women Must Suffer

In Genesis, Eve, the prototypical woman, sinned and invited Adam to sin. Thus Eve—and through her all women—are condemned to suffer in childbirth, so the story goes. But not solely in childbirth: from the moment of Eve's sin forward, women must expect to suffer in multiple ways. John Bunyan's *The Pilgrim's Progress*, a seventeenth-century best-selling devotional manual, narrates Christian's pilgrimage to the Celestial City. At the beginning of his journey, the Interpreter instructs Christian in how to be a Christian: he outfits Christian in head-to-toe armor, gives him weapons, and teaches him to fight. When Christiana begins her journey some time later, the Interpreter shows her how to live a Christian life. He takes her to a shed where sheep are being slaughtered and tells her that the Christian life for her is patient suffering: "See how patiently this sheep meets her death; without complaint she allows her skin to be pulled over her ears."

---

19. Brock and Parker, *Saving Paradise*.

Recollections and Reconsiderations

Identification of an Enemy

From devotional manuals to imperial decrees the identification of an opponent against whom to focus has been crucial to the project of unity. In the history of Christianity, "nothing is more precious than an enemy."[20] The closer the enemy, the better. In the early centuries of the common era, when Christians faced erratic but persistent persecution, the Roman state was the enemy; no other was needed. A bit later, patristic authors agree that not death but *deadness* was the enemy of the *life* Christ brought to believers. Numerous enemies have been proposed through the history of Christianity, but none more consistently and loudly than "the flesh."[21]

3

Fragile, intelligent mortal bodies, committed to participation in the "Body of Christ," may yet rediscover the most underdeveloped Christian doctrine, the Incarnation of Christ. Christ's incarnation declares a "collapse into immediacy"[22] of the God constructed and projected by theologians.[23] In bringing divinity to a human body, Christ's Incarnation brought divinity to all human bodies. Largely owing to a dominant philosophical anthropology that belittles or neglects body *as religiously insignificant*, the Incarnation has remained a belief, boldly asserted but abstract. Christianity has focused on soul, spirituality, and another world, rather than our beautiful and endangered world of living intelligent bodies. It is rapidly becoming evident that we cannot maintain this tragic trajectory. Prompted by Christ's Incarnation, we must now rethink, revalue, remember, and love *this* world, the world of bodies and senses.

---

20. Sheets-Johnstone, quoting D. Shulman: *Insides and Outsides*, 28.

21. Paul's use of "flesh" as synecdoche for the whole person under sin, but literalized by generations of Christians, is well discussed by J. A. T. Robinson, *The Body*.

22. R. G. Collingwood's phrase in *The Idea of History*.

23. See Marion for a critique of "the 'God' constructed and projected by theologians," *God Without Being*.

Chapter 10

"My Weight Is My Love"

1

For a number of years, Gordon Kaufman, my colleague at Harvard Divinity School, and I had an ongoing discussion about the difference between theology and religion. I claimed that theology should *tell* everything one knows religiously. Gordon said that theology is about thinking and religion is about praying—two very different activities. Theology must meet Wittgenstein's standard, "Everything that can be said can be said clearly."[1] Everything that can be known religiously, however, cannot be said clearly. As Simeon the New Theologian of Eastern Orthodoxy (d. 1022) wrote:

> Do not try to express ineffable matters by words alone, for this is an impossibility. But let us contemplate such matters by activity, labor, and fatigue. In this way we shall be taught the meaning of such things as the sacred mysteries.[2]

"Words alone" cannot describe religious experience. The twentieth-century poet Robert Creeley wrote despairingly, "Words, words, as if all worlds were there." Religious understanding must be the result of *practice*: "activity, labor, and fatigue"—life. But shared experience, shared *participation*,

---

1. Wittgenstein, *Tractatus Logico Philosophicus*, 4.116
2. Simeon the New Theologian, *Orations*, 26.

does not need to be analyzed and articulated. "Do *this* in remembrance of me"—"*do this*"—not "believe this" or "recite these words."

But theology's medium is "words alone." Theology analyzes and articulates, at best explaining religious experience to "cultured despisers."[3] It is too late to give Gordon Kaufman the satisfaction of conceding his point, but I must do just that. Theology and religious experience have different *modus operandi*. Short of experience, words, though not ideal, are *all we have*. So I continue to struggle to say what I mean, appreciating enormously when someone seems to understand what I'm *trying* to say.

2

Powerful as Augustine's advocacy of love has been and *is* for me, I have needed further help for the love project to "collapse into immediacy" in my life. Augustine the theologian, described beautifully what a Christian life most essentially *is*, namely, a person who is becoming loving. But I have needed more practical help than he gives—or can give with "words alone." For this I am indebted both to liturgical practice—participation—and to the clinical method of a twentieth-century psychoanalyst, Sigmund Freud.

Augustine said that a person is defined by the objects of her attention and affection, her love. "My weight is my love," he said, "by it I am carried wherever I am carried."[4] The sixteenth-century Dominican priest, St. John of the Cross, wrote, "In everything you love and fear you will find yourself there." Freud claimed that a person is defined by his fear. According to these authors, love and fear are the two passions powerful enough to become a person's "weight," and thus to define her.

Augustine frequently quoted 1 John 4:18: "There is no fear in love for perfect love casts out fear." But who has perfect love without any admixture of fear? And fear, in sufficient strength, can effectively preclude and cancel love. Love is a *process*, a journey between a commitment and a goal, not an attitude or a feeling that one can simply adopt. Augustine and Freud agreed that fear can be overcome, but they had different recommendations for overcoming it.

Augustine suggested that in the minutia of everyday life one should focus on *localizing* and *particularizing* love, on acting lovingly. As attention and energy are placed on "carrying over" psychic weight to love, fear will

---

3. Schleiermacher's term.
4. Augustine, *Confessions*, 13.9.

necessarily and automatically be diminished. But Augustine did not specify *how* fear can become love, except to recommend petitioning God for help. He simply states the commandment: "We are bidden to take away from the weight of *cupiditas* and add to the weight of *caritas* until the former vanish and the latter be perfected."[5] The method and goal, he says, are the same: "The way you are going is the same as the 'whither' you are going."[6] Augustine *loads* the activity of augmenting love into the practice of everyday life.

But a problem arises: Christians like to think of ourselves as loving, so we often ignore, mask, or actively disavow the extent to which we are directed, not by love but by fear. Because our *conscious intention* is to love, we think we act lovingly. Ironically, by denying our fear, we foreclose the possibility of imitating the loving Christ. Forgotten, denied, or unconscious fear is *acted out*. Unacknowledged fear expresses itself in seeking scapegoats to explain our fear (to ourselves) and rationalize it (to others. There is a more complex relationship between fear and love than the First John passage indicates. Freud suggests that we can increase in love *only* by recognizing and acknowledging our fears *in order to redeem and redirect their energy*.

Freud proposed a *method* for "carrying over" the weight of fear to love. Unlike Augustine's recommendation that we concentrate on *acting lovingly*, Freud recommended that a person bring her fear to consciousness, that she *spell out*—discover, acknowledge, and relive—her fear. The slow, patient work of psychoanalysis brings fear to consciousness where it is stripped of its power. The "talking cure" can free the psyche from the strangling grip of fear, producing the capacity for love and work, Freud's criteria for psychic health.

Augustine claimed to be motivated completely by love—"by it I am carried wherever I am carried." But Augustine "thought he was perfect because his conscious intention was perfect."[7] He ignored the many fears noticed by readers of his *Confessions*—from fear of readers' ridicule to fear of displeasing his God.[8] Augustine's theology of love did not alter his contentious campaigns against the "monsters" who opposed his interpretations of Christian doctrine. His last controversy (with Julian of Eclanum) was

---

5. Augustine, *De doctrina christiana*, 3.10.
6. Augustine, *In Iohannis evangelium*, 13.4.
7. Milner, "Psychoanalysis and Art," 86.
8. Augustine, *In Ps.* CXVIII, *Serm*, 25, 7; *Ep.*, CXL 21.53. In later writings, Augustine acknowledged that he "trembled" in relation to pastoral decisions. He even recognized a valuable kind of fear that he called "chaste fear." Servile fear dreads punishment, Augustine preached, while chaste fear only fears being abandoned by God.

more rancorous than ever. He needed a method for uncovering the sources of his anger in his fears.[9]

I have needed the advice of both Augustine and Freud. I have needed Augustine for incentive and energy—*inardescimus et imus*—and I have needed Freud to describe the necessary commitment to a plodding, slow, undramatic method by which to "take away from fear and add to love."[10]

3

We want to feel "truly alive,"[11] and safety and comfort are the identified enemies of a sharp, strong sense of life.[12] We would *like* to "have it all now"—comfort, safety, *and* a strong feeling of aliveness—but we must juggle conflicting needs every day. We need *enough* safety to be able to take the risks that give us a feeling of aliveness. Most of us err either in seeking too much safety or in opting for more risk than our fragile psyches can support. Rarely, and briefly, we get the balance just right.

In a cemetery on the Greek island of Paros, I found in a box of bones an icon that had petrified into a sternum. Presumably the sternum's owner had worn the icon all his life and continued to wear it in death. This image became for me a metaphor of Augustine's words, ossified into my bones and defining my life intention: "We are bidden to take away from the weight of *cupiditas* [anxious grasping in the fear that something will be missed], and add to the weight of *caritas* [love] until the former vanish and the latter be perfected."[13] This is my conscious intention, but I am sure that, like Augustine's readers, my readers will notice the irruption into my text of other, less worthy, agenda as well. I cannot in honesty say with the forty-year old Augustine, "My weight is my love, by it I am carried wherever I am carried."[14]

---

9. In his controversy with Julian he was led apparently in desperation—to identify conception as the moment in which original sin was transmitted, an identification with lasting and unfortunate consequences.

10. I am the grateful beneficiary of many hours of psychotherapy.

11. A fourth-century Eucharistic prayer attributed to Serapion of Thmuis (in Egypt) reads, "We beg you, make us truly alive"; see also my book, *Fullness of Life* for a discussion of patristic authors' claim that one of the gifts of Christ's incarnation was that he brought life to humans.

12. "My Dinner with André."

13. Augustine, *De doctrina Chrisiana*, 3.10.

14. Augustine, *Confessions*, 13.9.

"My Weight Is My Love"

Perhaps, for Augustine as for me, this was a goal, not a "perfected" reality. Meantime, as Pascal wrote, "I live joyously."[15]

This is the story I tell myself about the core and trajectory of my life.

> *If, then, the truest life is life by thought,*
>   *and is the same as the truest thought,*
>   *then the truest thought lives,*
> *and contemplation, and the object of contemplation*
>   *at this level, is living and life,*
> *and the two together are one.*[16]

---

15. Pascal, *Pensées*, # 793.
16. Plotinus, *Enneads*, 3.8.3.

Bibliography

Unless I have used a particular translation, I have not indicated translations for historical works for which there are many translations.

Arendt, Hannah. *Eichmann in Jerusalem*. New York: Kino International, 1999.
———. *The Life of the Mind*. Vol. 1, *Thinking*. New York: Harcourt, Brace, and Javanovich, 1971.
Aristotle. *Nichomachean Ethics*.
Astell, Ann W. *Eating Beauty: The Eucharist and the Spiritual Arts of the Middle Ages*. Ithaca, New York: Cornell University Press, 2006.
Augustine. *De civitate dei*.
———. *Confessions*, Transl. Rex Warner. New York: Mentor Omega, 1963.
———. *De catechizandis rudibus*.
———. *De doctrina christiana*.
———. *De trinitate*.
———. *Epistula*.
———. *Retractationes*. *The Fathers of the Church*. Washington DC: Catholic University of America Press, 1968.
———. *Sermons*.
Barthes, Roland. *The Pleasure of the Text*. Richard Miller, transl. New York: Hill and Wang, 1975.
Baxandall, Michael. *Painting and Experience in Fifteenth Century Italy*. New York: Oxford University Press, 1972.
Bonner, Gerald. "*Libido* and *Concupiscentia* in St. Augustine." *Studia Patristica* 6 (1962).
Brock, Rita Nakashima, and Rebecca Parker. *Saving Paradise*. Boston: Beacon, 2008.
Brown, Peter. *Augustine of Hippo: A Biography*, second ed. Berkeley: University of California Press, 2000.
Bunyan, John. *The Pilgrim's Progress*.
Burrus, Virginia, Mark D. Jordan, and Karmen Mackendrick, eds. *Seducing Augustine Bodies, Desires, Confessions*. New York: Fordham University Press, 2010.
Collingwood, R. G. *The Idea of History*. Oxford: Clarendon Press, 1949.
Davidson, Arnold. *The Emergence of Sexuality: Historical Epistemology and the Formation of Concepts*. Cambridge MA: Harvard University Press, 2001.
Descartes, *Discourse on the Method*.

Bibliography

Dreyfus and Rabinow. *Michel Foucault: Beyond Structuralism and Hermeneutics.* Chicago: University of Chicago Press, 1983.
Epic of Gilgamesh.
Fingarette, Herbert. *Self Deception,* 2nd edition. Berkeley: University of California Press, 2000.
Freud, Sigmund. *Civilization and Its Discontents.* London: Hogarth, 1930.
Gallop, Jane. *The Daughter's Seduction.* New York: Cornell University Press, 1982.
Greenblatt, Stephen. "The Invention of Sex." *The New Yorker* (June 19, 2017) 283–95.
Haraway, Donna. *Writing on the Body.* New York: State University of New York Press, 1997.
Harrison, Carol. *Augustine: Christian Faith and Fractured Humanity* . New York: Oxford University Press, 2000.
Hustvedt, Siri. *The Sorrows of an American.* New York: Henry Holt, 2008.
James, William. *The Varieties of Religious Experience.* Centenary edition. New York: Routledge, 2002.
Lexicon Plotinianum. J.H. Sleeman and Gilbert Pollet, eds. Leuven University Press, 1980.
Lossky, Vladimir. *The Mystical Theology of the Eastern Church.* St. Vladimir's Seminary Press, 1976.
Luther, Martin. *Lectures on Jonah. Luther's Works,* vol. 19. St. Louis: Concordia, 1975.
———. *Magnificat. Luther's Works,* vol. 21. St. Louis: Concordia, 1968.
Marion, Jean-Luc. *God Without Being.* Thomas A. Carlson, trans. Chicago: University of Chicago Press, 1991.
McGrath, Patrick. *Trauma.* New York: Knopf, 2008.
Milner, Marion. "Psychoanalysis and Art." In *Psychoanalysis and Art.* Sandra Grosso, ed. New York: Karmac, 2004.
Miles, Margaret R. "Achieving the Christian Body: Visual Incentives to Imitation of Christ in the Christian West." In *Interpreting Christian Art: Reflections on Christian Art,* edited by Heidi Hornik and Mikeal Parsons. Macon, GA: Mercer University Press, 2004.
———. *Agostino Confessioni.* Turin, Italy: Lindau, 1991.
———. "Art, Gender and Religion." In *The Cambridge Companion to Art and Religion,* edited by Frank Burch Brown, 469–79. Cambridge: Cambridge University Press, 2014.
———. "Art and Liturgy: Cooperation or Competition?" *Faith and Form* XIX (Spring, 1986) 10–12.
———. *Augustine on the Body.* Missoula, MT: Scholars, 1979.
———. *Augustine and the Fundamentalist's Daughter.* Eugene, OR: Cascade, 2011.
———. "Augustine and Freud: The Secularization of Self-Deception." In *Augustine and Psychology,* edited by Kim Paffenroth, Robert P. Kennedy, John Doody, 115–30. Lantham, MD: Lexington Books, 2012.
———. "Augustine Reading and Reading Augustine." *The Christian Century,* Vol. 114, #15 (May 1997).
———. "Becoming Answerable for What We See" (1999 Presidential Address, American Academy of Religion). *Journal Of The American Academy Of Religion,* Vol. 68 #3 (Fall 2000) 471–85.
———. *Beyond the Centaur: Imagining the Intelligent Body.* Eugene, OR: Cascade, 2017.
———. *Bodies in Society: Essays on Christianity in Contemporary Culture.* Eugene, OR: Cascade, 2008.

Bibliography

———. "The Body and Human Values in Augustine of Hippo." *Augustinian Heritage* Vol. 33:1 (1987) 57–70.

———. "The Body and Human Values in Augustine of Hippo." In *Grace, Politics, and Desire: Essays on Augustine*. University of Calgary, 1990, 55–70.

———. "Carnal Abominations: The Female Body as Grotesque." In *The Grotesque in Art and Literature*, edited by James Luther Adams and Wilson Yates. New York: Eerdmans, 1997.

———. *A Complex Delight: The Secularization of the Breast, 1350–1750*. Berkeley, CA: University of California Press, 2008.

———. "The Courage to be Alone, In and Out of Marriage." In *The Feminist Mystic and Other Essays on Women and Spirituality*, edited by Mary Giles. New York: Crossroad, 1982.

———. *Desire and Delight: A New Reading of Augustine's Confessions*. Eugene, OR: Wipf and Stock, 2006.

———. "Disney Spirituality: An Oxymoron?" In *Riding on Faith: Essays on Religion, Culture and the World of Disney*, edited by Laurie Zoloth and Simon Harek. American Academy of Religion: Religion and Culture Series, 1999.

———. "The Eye of the Beholder." In *The Subjective Eye: Essays in Culture, Religion, and Gender in honor of Margaret R. Miles*, edited by Richard Valantasis, xix–xxix. Eugene, OR: Princeton Theological Monograph Series, Pickwick Publications, 2006.

———. "Facie ad faciem: Visuality, Desire, and the Discourse of the Other." *Journal of Religion*, Vol. 87 #1 (January 2007) 43–58.

———. "Fashioning the Self." *The Christian Century*, Vol.112 #8 (March 8, 1995) 273–75.

———. "Favorite Books and How They Influence." *The Christian Century*, Vol.104, #17 (May 20–27, 1987) 490–95.

———. "A Feminine Figure in Christian Tradition: Conversation with Luce Irigaray, Laine M. Harrington, and Margaret R. Miles." *Conversations with Luce Irigaray*, 85–106. London: Continuum, 2008.

———. "From Rape to Resurrection: Sin, Sexual Difference and Politics." In *Augustine's City of God: A Critical Guide*, edited by James Wetzel, 75–92. New York: Cambridge University Press, 2012.

———. *Fullness of Life: Historical Foundations for a New Asceticism*. Louisville: Westminster, 1981.

———. *Getting Here from There: Conversations on Life and Work*. Eugene, OR: Cascade, 2011.

———. "God's Love, Mother's Milk." *The Christian Century*, Vol.125 #2 (January 29, 2008) 22–26.

———. "Happiness in Motion: Desire and Delight." In *In Pursuit of Happiness: Boston University Studies in Philosophy and Religion*, XVI, 38–56. Notre Dame: University of Notre Dame Press, 1995.

———. "Hermeneutics of Generosity and Suspicion: Theological Education in a Pluralistic Setting." *Theological Education* XIII (Supplement, 1987) 34–52.

———. "Hospitable Vision: Some Notes on the Ethics of Seeing Film." With Brent Plate. *Crosscurrents*, Vol. 54 #1 (Spring 2004) 22–31.

———. *The Image and Practice of Holiness*. Reprint. Eugene, OR: Wipf and Stock, 2006.

———. "Image." In *Critical Terms for Religious Studies*, edited by Mark C. Taylor. Chicago: University of Chicago Press, 1997.

BIBLIOGRAPHY

———. *Image as Insight, Visual Understanding in Western Christianity and Secular Culture*. Boston: Beacon, 1985.

———. "Imitation of Christ: Is it Possible in the Twentieth Century?" *The Princeton Seminary Bulletin*, Vol. X:1 (1989) 7–22.

———. "Infancy, Parenting and Nourishment in Augustine's *Confessions*." In *The Hunger of the Heart: Reflections on the Confessions of Augustine*, edited by Donald Capps, and James E. Dittes, 296–36. West Lafayette, IN: Society for the Scientific Study of Religion Monograph Series, 1991.

———. "Infancy, Parenting, and Nourishment in Augustine's *Confessions*." *Journal of the American Academy of Religion* (September, 1982) 349–64.

———. "Introduction." In *Immaculate and Powerful, The Female in Sacred Image and Social Reality*, edited by Clarissa W. Atkinson, Constance H. Buchanan, and Margaret R. Miles. Boston: Beacon, 1985.

———. "Introduction." In *Priests, Sex, and Power: Anatomy of a Crisis*, A.W. Richard Sipe, ix–xiv. New York: Brunner-Routledge, 1995.

———. "'Jesus Patabilis': Augustine's Debate with the Manichaeans." In *Faithful Imagining: Essays in Honor of Richard R. Niebuhr*, edited by Sang Lee and Wayne Proudfoot, 3–18. Atlanta: Scholars, 1995.

———. "Larry Flynt in Real Life." *The Christian Century*, Vol. 114, #14 (April 1997) 419–20.

———. "Living Lovingly in a Culture of Fear." In *I Have Called You Friends: Reflections on Reconciliation in Honor of Frank T. Griswold*, edited by Barbara Braver, 179–90. Cambridge: Cowley, 2006.

———. *The Long Goodbye: Dementia Diaries*. Eugene, OR: Wipf and Stock, 2014.

———. "Making Historical Theology." In *Christian Thought in the 21st Century: Agenda for the Future*, edited by Douglas H. Shanz, Tinu Ruparell, 48–51. University of Calgary Press, 2000.

———. "The Mystical Method of Meister Eckhart." *Studia Mystica* IV:4 (Winter 1981) 57–71.

———. "North African Christianity in the Roman Period." In *African Spirituality: Forms, Meanings, and Expressions*, edited by Jacob Olupona, 350–71. World Spirituality Series, Vol. 3. New York: Crossroad, 2000.

———. "Not Nameless but Unnamed: The Woman Torn from Augustine's Side." In *Feminist Interpretations of Augustine*, edited by Judith Stark, 167–88. University Park, PA: Pennsylvania State University Press, 2007.

———. "Nudity, Gender, and Religious Meaning in the Italian Renaissance." *Art as Religious Studies*, edited by Diane Apostolos-Cappadona, and Doug Adams, 101–16. New York: Crossroad, 1987.

———. "Passion for Social Justice and 'The Passion of the Christ.'" In *Mel Gibson's Bible: Religion, Popula Culture, and "The Passion of the Christ,"* edited by Timothy K. Beal, and Tod Linafelt, 121–28. Chicago: University of Chicago Press, 2005.

———. "Patriarchy as Political Theology: The Establishment of North African Christianity." In *Civil Religion and Political Theology, Boston University Studies in Philosophy and Religion*, Vol. VIII, edited by Leroy Rouner. Notre Dame, IN: University of Notre Dame Press, 1986.

———. "Pilgrimage as Metaphor in a Nuclear Age." *Theology Today*, Vol. XLV, #2 (July, 1988) 166–79.

Bibliography

———. *Plotinus on Body and Beauty: Society, Philosophy, and Religion in the Third Century*. Hoboken, NJ: Blackwell, 1999.

———. *Practicing Christianity: Critical Perspectives for an Embodied Spirituality*. New York: Crossroad, 1988.

———. "The Pursuit of Lifefulness: In Search of a Method." *Studia Mystica* VII: 4 (Winter, 1984) 63–69.

———. *Reading for life: Beauty, Pluralism, and Responsibility*. New York: Continuum, 1997.

———. "Reading For Life: Hermeneutics of Generosity and Suspicion." *Sewanee Theological Review*, Vol. XLI (Christmas 1997) 19–58.

———. "The Recovery of Asceticism." *Commonweal* (28 January 1983) 40.

———. "El redescubrimiento del asceticismo." *Criterio* LVI (28 July 1983).

———. "Religion and Food: The Case of Eating Disorders." *Journal of the American Academy of Religion* Vol. LXIII (Fall 1995) 549–64.

———. *Rereading Historical Theology: Before, During, and After Augustine*. Eugene, OR: Cascade, 2008.

———. "Response to Reviews of *Augustine and the Fundamentalist's Daughter*." *Pastoral Psychology*, Vol. 62#3 (June 2013) 393–98.

———. "The Resurrection of Body: Re-imagining Human Personhood in the Christian Tradition." In *Theology Aesthetics, and Culture: Responses to the Work of David Brown*, edited by Robert McSwain and Taylor Worley, 42–52. Oxford: Oxford University Press, 2012.

———. "The Revelatory Body: Signorelli's *Resurrection of the Flesh* at Orvieto." *Theological Education*, Vol. XXXI #1 (Autumn 1994) 75–90.

———. "'The Rope Breaks When It Is Tightest': Luther on the Body, Consciousness, and the Word." *Harvard Theological Review* Vol. 77:3–4 (1984) 239–58.

———. "Rouault and the Dynamics of Self-Deception." In *Mystic Masque: Semblance and Reality in Georges Rouault*, edited by Stephan Schloesser, 109–16. Boston: McMullen Museum of Art, Boston College, 2008.

———. "Santa Maria Maggiore's Fifth-Century Mosaics: Triumphal Christianity and the Jews." *Harvard Theological Review*, Vol. 86:2 (April 1993) 155–72.

———. "A Sea of Love: Marguerite Porete's *A Mirror for Simple Souls*," *The Christian Century*, Vol. 110 #4 (February 3–10, 1993).

———. *Seeing and Believing: Religion and Values in the Movies*. Boston: Beacon, 1997.

———. "Seeing is Believing: Shinjo Ito and the Role of Vision in Religious Practice." In *The Vision and Art of Shinjo Ito*, edited by Mark Robinson, 15–24. Firenze, Italy: Alinari, 2008.

———. "Sex and the City (of God): Is Sex Forfeited or fulfilled in Augustine's Resurrection of Body?" *Journal of the American Academy of Religion*, Vol. 73/2 (June 2005) 307–27.

———. *Shaping New Vision: Gender and Values in American Culture*. Edited by Clarissa W. Atkinson, Constance H. Buchanan and Margaret R. Miles, eds. Ann Harbor: UMI, 1987.

———. "Tasteless Historical Stories: An Historical Theologian's Responsibility to Past and Present." In *Responsibility*, edited by Barbara Darling-Smith. Boston University Studies in Philosophy and Religion XXVI. Notre Dame, IN: University of Notre Dame Press, 2005

———. "Temor y amor en san Augustin." *Augustinus* Vol. 26 (July-December, 1981).

BIBLIOGRAPHY

———. "Textual Harassment: Desire and the Female Body." In *The Good Body: Asceticism in Contemporary Culture,* edited by Mary G. Winkler, Letha B. Cole, 49–63. New Haven: Yale University Press, 1994.

———. "Theology, Anthropology, and the Human Body in Calvin's *Institutes of Christian Religion.*" *Harvard Theological Review* (July, 1981) 303.

———. "Theory, Theology, and Episcopal Church Women." In *Women of the Protestant Mainline: A Case Study of the Episcopal Church in the Twentieth Century,* edited by Catherine Prelinger, 330–44. Oxford: Oxford University Press, 1992.

———. "Toward a New Asceticism." *The Christian Century* (14 October 1981) 1097–98.

———. "Violence Against Women in the Historical Christian West and in North American Secular Culture: The Visual and Textual Evidence." In *Shaping New Vision: Gender and Values in American Culture.* Ann Arbor: UMI Research Press, 1987.

———. "The Virgin's One Bare Breast: Female Nudity and Religious Meaning in Renaissance Culture." In *The Expanding Discourse: Feminism and Art History,* edited by Norma Broude, and Mary D. Garrard, . New York: Harper Collins, 1992.

———. "The Virgin's One Bare Breast: Female Nudity and Religious Meaning in Renaissance Culture." In *The Female Body in Western Culture: Contemporary Perspectives,* edited by Susan Rubin Suleiman, 193–203. Cambridge, MA: Harvard University Press, 1986.

———. "A Vision of Feminist Religious Scholarship." *Journal of Feminist Studies in Religion,* Vol.3:1(Spring, 1987) 91–111.

———. "Vision: The Eye of the Body and the Eye of the Mind in Saint Augustine's *De trinitate* and *Confessions.*" *Journal of Religion* Vol. 63, #2 (April 1983) 125–42.

———. "Voyeurism and Visual Images of Violence." *The Christian Century* (March 1984) 305-6.

———. *The Wendell Cocktail: Depression, Addiction, and Beauty.* Eugene, OR: Cascade, 2012.

———. "What You See Is What You Get: Religion on Primetime Fiction Television." In *Religion and Primetime Fiction Television,* edited by Michael Suman, 37–46. Thousand Oaks, CA: Sage, 1997.

———. "*Winged Figure* and Rilke's Islamic Angels in the *Duino Elegies.*" *Arts in Religious and Theological Studies,* Vol 22 #1 (2010), 43–47.

———. *The Word Made Flesh: A History of Christian Thought.* Hoboken, NJ: Blackwell, 2005.

———. "The Word Made Flesh: Toward a Feminist History of Christian Thought." *The Journal of Feminist Studies in Religion,* Spring 2006

Morrison, Toni. *Jazz.* New York: Knopf, *1992.*

Murdoch, Iris. *Metaphysics as a Guide to Morals.* New York: Penguin, 1993.

Nicene and Post-Nicene Fathers, edited by Philip Schaff. Peabody, MA 1994

O'Connell, Robert J. *Augustine's Early Theory of Man,* 386–391. Cambridge, MA: Harvard University Press, 1968.

O'Donnell, James. *Augustine, Sinner and Saint: A New Biography.* London: Profile Books, 2005.

Pascal, Blaise. *Pensées.*

Plato. *Collected Dialogues,* Edith Hamilton and Huntington Cairns, eds. Princeton: Princeton University Press, 1961.

Plotinus, *The Enneads,* 7 vols. Transl A. H. Armstrong. Loeb Classical Library. Cambridge MA: Harvard University Press, 1966–88.

Bibliography

Robinson, J.A.T. *The Body: A Study in Pauline Theology.* London: SCM, 1952.
Rogoff, Irit. "Tiny Anguished Reflections on Nagging, Scholastic Embarrassment, and Feminist Art History." *Differences* 4, no. 3 (1992).
Rousseau, *Confessions.*
Sanday, Peggy Reeves. *Female Power and Male Dominance: On the Origins of Sexual Inequality.* New York: Cambridge University Press, 1981.
Sheets-Johnstone, Maxine. *Insides and Outsides.* Boston: Beacon, 2016..
———. *The Corporeal Turn: An Interdisciplinary Reader.* Exeter: Imprint Academic, 2009.
Tertullian. *De anima.*
Traherne, Thomas. *Centuries of Meditation.* London: Dobell, 1948.
Trinkhaus, Charles and Heiko A. Overmann. *The Pursuit of Holiness in Late Medieval and Renaissance Religion.* Leiden: E.J. Brill, 1974.
Williams, Norman Powell. *Ideas of the Fall and of Original Sin.* London: Longmans, Green, 1927.
Valantasis, Richard. *Dazzling Bodies: Rethinking Spirituality and Community Formation.* Eugene, OR: Cascade, 2014.
Wittgenstein, Ludwig. *Tractus Logico Philosophicus.*
Young, Iris Marrion. *Justice and the Politics of Difference.* Princeton: Princeton University Press, 2011.

Index

Academic institutions, 86–88
American Academy of Religion, 80
asceticism, 19–22
Arendt, Hannah, 6, 23
Aristotle, 73
"Art, Gender, and Religion", 118–19
Augustine (of Hippo)
  body, 15, 18
  City of God, 111–12
  Confessions, 11, 57–58, 60–62, 127, 145
  and Freud, 111–12, 145
  happiness, 69–70
  love, 144
  Retractationes, 125–27
  Roman North Africa, 42–43
  unhappiness, 48
  women, 99–100
autobiography, 106–8
  Augustine and the Fundamentalist's Daughter, 108–10
  The Long Goodbye, 120–21

beauty, 77, 81, 100–101
Bellow, Saul, 117
Beowulf, 120
body (the), 5, 15, 18
  eye of, 30
  female, 67, 76
  Christian, 92
  Incarnation, 142
Bonhoeffer, 91–92
breast, secularization, 104
Brown, David, 114–15
Brown, Peter, 11

Buddhism, 102–3
Bunyan, John (*The Pilgrim's Progress*), 141

Calvin, 21–22
catechisms (16th-century Lutheran), 33–34
celibacy, 71–72
competition and cooperation, 58–60
concupiscentia, 27–28
conversion, 138–39
Cooper, Anna Julia, 7n22
critical approach, 6
councils, ecumenical
  Chalcedon (451 CE), 95
  Ephesus (431 CE), 56
  Second Council of Nicaea (CE787), 132–33
  Fourth Lateran (1215 CE), 137–38

Davidson, Arnold, 16
death, 17
Descartes, 105
cevotional manuals, 52–54

Eastern Orthodoxy, 132–33
Eckhart, 22–23
enemy, 53, 142
Episcopal Church women, 62–63
Eucharist, 137–38

fear, 98, 145
feminist history, 98–99
Festschrift, 97
film, 75, 78,

Index

Fingarette, Herbert, 112–14
food, 70–71
Foucault, Michel, 37, 24, 41, 55, 131
Freud, Sigmund, 57, 112–14, 145

Gallop, Jane, 11
Gibson, Mel ("The Passion of the Christ"), 96
Graduate Theological Union, 74–75
Greenblatt, Stephan, 130
Gregory Palamas, 54

happiness, 69–70
Harrington, Laine, 103–4
Harvard University Divinity School, 13, 25–26, 94
　Harvard Women's Studies in Religion, 44, 46–47
historiography, 8–9, 36
Hunt, Lynn, *Inventing Human Rights*, 78

idolatry
　icons, 132
　language, 133–34
images, 36–37, 104
　breast, (BVM), 43, 140–41
　crucifixion, 140
"intelligent body", 21, 23, 115, 119
Irigaray, Luce, 103
Isenheim Altarpiece, 32

James, William, 138–39
Jews, 65–67
Jonah, xi–xii
Jovinian, 128

Kaufman, Gordon, 143

Langer, Suzanne, 109
language, 8, 36–37, 128, 132–34
love, 145ff.
Luther, Martin, xi–xii, 33, 52

Manichaeans, 68
media, and religion, 72, 79, 98
mental illness, 116–17

Miles, Wendell (*The Wendell Cocktail*), 116
Miller, Arthur, 24
"My Dinner with André", 31–32

nakedness, female, 55–56
non-Chalcedonian churches, 95
novels, 109
nuclear world, 50

objectivity, 17
O'Donnell, James, 4, 125, 128
original sin, 56n26, 129, 130

pilgrimage, 50–51
Pilgrim's Progress (The), 51, 141
Plato/Platonism, 16, 18, 73,
Plotinus, xii, 7, 8, 80
　On Body and Beauty, 81–86
pluralism (in theological education), 49
Porete, Marguerite, 67
practice (of Christianity), 143
psychotherapy, 7, 146n10
predestination (Calvin), 21–22
　Augustine, 129

relationship, 24
resurrection (of body), 16–17, 93, 111–12, 114–15
Riefenstahl, Leni, 76–77
Rilke, *Letters to a Young Poet*, 76–77
Rockefeller Center, Bellagio, Italy, 28–29
Roman North Africa, 42–43
Rouault, Georges, 101
Rousseau, Jean-Jacques, 6

"safe space", 59–60
Sakamura, Hiroko, *Getting Here from There*, 110–11
Sanday, Peggy Reeves, 45
Santa Maria Maggiore, mosaics, 65
self-consistency, 6
self-deception, 101–2, 112–14
sex (in the resurrection), 93–94, 111–12
Sheets-Johnstone, Maxine, 18

Index

Shinjo Ito, Shinnyo-en Buddhism, 102–3
Signorelli ("Resurrection of the Flesh," Orvieto, Italy), 64–65
Simeon, the New Theologian, 143
soul, 134–35
suffering, 141

"Tasteless Historical Stories", 94
teaching, 13–15, 91
Tertullian, 56
textbook (*The Word Made Flesh*), 94

Theotokos, BVM, 56
Traherne, Thomas, 114n16, 120n21

"unity", 135–38

violence, 32, 45ff, 78–79

Williams, George Hunston, 13
women's history, 98–99, 141

Young, Iris Marion, 136–38

www.ingramcontent.com/pod-product-compliance
Lightning Source LLC
Chambersburg PA
CBHW030115170426
43198CB00009B/628